Business Explorer 1

Student's Book

Gareth Knight
Mark O'Neil

CAMBRIDGE
UNIVERSITY PRESS

PUBLISHED BY THE PRESS SYNDICATE OF THE UNIVERSITY OF CAMBRIDGE
The Pitt Building, Trumpington Street, Cambridge, United Kingdom

CAMBRIDGE UNIVERSITY PRESS
The Edinburgh Building, Cambridge CB2 2RU, UK
40 West 20th Street, New York, NY 10011–4211, USA
10 Stamford Road, Oakleigh, Melbourne 3166, Australia
Ruiz de Alarcón 13, 28014 Madrid, Spain
Dock House, The Waterfront, Cape Town 8001, South Africa
http://www.cambridge.org

First published 2001

Designed by Harris Design Associates, page make-up by Hart Mcleod

Printed in the United Kingdom at the University Press, Cambridge

ISBN 0 521 77780 1   Student's Book
ISBN 0 521 77779 8   Teacher's Book
ISBN 0 521 77778 X   Audio Cassette
ISBN 0 521 77777 1   Audio CD

Contents

Map of the book

New faces

UNIT GOALS
- introducing yourself
- talking about yourself
- introducing other people

TALKING POINT

Answer these questions yourself. Ask two of your classmates the same questions. Have you ...

- introduced yourself to one of the people in this room?
- ever introduced yourself to a customer or colleague?
- ever introduced someone else to a customer or colleague?

Part A Introducing yourself

1 Listening

Look at the photograph. Lucy Chang is introducing herself to Andrew Walsh. With a partner, answer these questions.

1 Which one do you think is a new employee?
2 Which person is from Human Resources?
3 Which of these topics will they talk about?

    names   interests   colleges   work   hometowns   ages   departments

Now listen to Lucy Chang and Andrew Walsh introducing themselves. What topics do they talk about? Were you right?

2 Language focus

a Andrew Walsh introduced himself. Complete the phrases he said.
1 My .... Andrew Walsh.
2 .... Phoenix, Arizona.
3 .... looking forward to ....

b Lucy Chang introduced herself. Complete the phrases she said.
1 .... Lucy Chang. .... Lucy.
2 .... the Human Resources Department.
3 .... in the Sales Department for six years.

 Listen again to check your answers.

3 Communication activity

Fill in the file card about yourself. Next, work with a partner to make sentences about each other. Then join another pair and tell them about your partner. Use the Help folder if you need to.

FILE CARD

Name .... From ....

School/College/University/Company/Department ....

....

Major/Job title ....

....

---

4 Culture focus

Lucy Chang told Andrew Walsh to call her 'Lucy' – her first name – not 'Ms. Chang' – her last name. What do you call the people you work with? Do you use the first name or the last name with a title?

CORPORATE INTERNATIONAL

MANAGER

LUCY CHANG

28 Bukit batok close, #17, Singapore 456766
Tel 65 4669 837 Fax 65 4669 838
Email customerservice@ci.co.sp

first name   last name

The situation is different around the world. Listen to three business people talking about the situation in their countries and answer the questions below.

1   How are names used in their countries?
2   Do they use first names, last names or other names when they speak to people?

1   Listening

a   Look at the photo of someone being introduced.
What do you think the people are saying?
Now listen to what the people say.

b   With a partner unscramble these phrases.

1   Mr. Haneda, / like / Joshua Travis / to / I'd / you / to / introduce / .
2   works / the / Joshua / Marketing / in / company / our / Division / of / .
3   Director / of / Mr. Haneda / is / Yonegawa Industries / a / .
4   to / you / meet / Nice / .
5   long / how / been / have / you / at / International foods / Mr. Travis / ?

Now listen again and check.

2   Language focus

Look at the stages of introducing two people. In groups of three, write examples for each stage.
Use your own names.

Person A   Person B   Person C

B introduces A and C by giving each person's name.

B adds extra information about A and C.

A and C use the information provided by B
to help start a conversation.

A tries to use C's name early in the conversation.   C tries to use A's name early in the conversation.

Example:

PERSON B: Mr. Haneda, I'd like to introduce you to Joshua
Travis. Joshua works in the Marketing Division of
our company.
Mr. Haneda is Director of Yonegawa Industries.

PERSON A: How long have you been at General foods,
Mr. Travis?

Useful language

How long have you been at ... (company)?
Which department do you work in?
How long have you been in ...
(department)?
Where are you from?

Culture focus

Read these questions and find the answers in the text below. Check your answers with a partner.

1 When a person is introduced, why is extra information about that person often added?
2 Why is it a good idea to use somebody's name immediately after being introduced?

When you first meet someone, you may have a short conversation before exchanging names. However, when you introduce two people, give their names at the beginning of the conversation and also add information about each person to help them talk to each other.

If you are introduced to someone, use their name immediately.
It will help you to remember it.

---

4   Communication activity

Work in groups of three. Choose a business card each and use the information to introduce yourselves to each other. Then introduce each other to another group. Add extra information about each other.

ダローバル商事

Junko Kawabata
SALES REPRESENTATIVE

Delta Systems Inc.

RICHARD HARVEY

DIRECTOR

Investments

Security

Somjai Nonchana
FINANCIAL MANAGER

UNIT 2

Around the office

UNIT GOALS
- talking about things in the office
- talking about work places and locations

 **TALKING POINT**

Which picture is like your office? Do any of these offices seem strange to you?

Which office would you not like to work in? Why?

Part A   In the office

1 Vocabulary

Look at the picture of an office in exercise 3 on page 11. Label the things you can see.

files.............................   ....

calculator.......................   ....

....

....

2 Listening

Sometimes you may need something but you don't know what it's called in English.

a   Listen to three conversations. What does the person want? Where is it? Draw a line. The first one is done for you.

Ruler	in the drawer
Hi-lite pen	on the desk
Notepad	in the cupboard
Whiteout	next to the paper
Eraser	next to the fax
Calculator	on the table

Useful language

It's for ...

It's stuff for ...

You use it to ...

It's a thing for ...

It's something we use to ...

In my language we call it ...

b   Think of three things in the office. Explain them to a partner using the language you heard in the listening. Does your partner know the word in English?

Your words   Your partner's words

1 ....   1 ....

2 ....   2 ....

3 ....   3 ....

3 Language focus

Work in pairs. Look at the picture and use the prepositions below to complete the sentences.

| next to | in | on | in front of | near | behind |

Example: The shelf is ..on.. the wall. There is a telephone ..on.. the desk.

1 There is a calculator .... the computer.
2 The computer disks are .... the shelf.
3 The .... is .... the window.
4 The .... is .... the computer.
5 The files are .... the filing cabinet.
6 The book is .... the computer.

Compare your answers with another pair.

4 Communication activity

STUDENT A: Look at the information on page 76.
STUDENT B: Look at the information below.

You have a picture of the same office as Student A, but there are ten small differences. Can you find them? Tell Student A about your picture and listen to Student A talk about his/hers.
Use the language in 3 Language focus to help you.

1 ....
2 ....
3 ....
4 ....
5 ....
6 ....
7 ....
8 ....
9 ....
10 ....

5 Exploring

Draw a plan of your office.
Explain your plan to a partner.
Now draw your partner's office.

Is there anything in your office would like to change? Why?

Your office	Your partner's office

1 Vocabulary

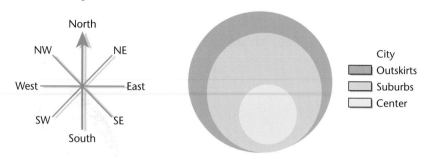

North
NW | NE
West —— East
SW | SE
South

City
☐ Outskirts
☐ Suburbs
☐ Center

Keiko Harada and Keiichi Yoneyama work in Tokyo, which is in the eastern part of Japan.

a Read about them and mark on the plan where they live and work.

Keiichi Yoneyama My home is in Tsukuba City which is about 100 km north of Tokyo. My office is in the outskirts in the eastern part of Tokyo.

Keiko Harada My office is in the Shinjuku area in the center of Tokyo. I live in the suburbs in the western part of Tokyo.

b Where do you live and work? Tell your partner.

2 Culture focus

a In many cities around the world, companies are moving to the outskirts of the city. Many workers are happy to live in the outskirts or in the country and drive to their new office. Is this happening in cities in your country?

b Ask your collegues where they would like to live and work and fill in the questionnaire.

(Would like) to live/work in the	center	suburbs	outskirts	countryside
Example: You	work	x	x	live

Now draw a rough map of your region. Mark their answers on the map.

c Where would you *not* like to live and work? Why not? Discuss with a partner.

3 Listening

Listen to someone talking about the location of Kanda Motors in Thailand. Check ☑ the work places the speaker talks about. Draw a line from the work place to the location on the map.

branch office ☐
factory ☐
warehouse ☐
showroom ☐
store ☐
design studio ☐
head office ☐

4 Communication activity

STUDENT A: Look at the information on page 76.
STUDENT B: Look at the information below.

Look at the maps of Shanghai and China below. The maps show the location of Fizco work places in China. Explain the locations to Student A.

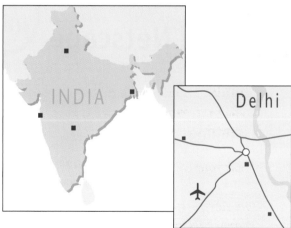

Now listen to Student A explain the locations of Fizco in India. Mark the locations on the maps above.

5 Writing

Work with a partner. Write a paragraph explaining the locations of your company. Then compare your paragraph with another pair.

Look at the Transcript on page 100 to help you.

Products and services

UNIT GOALS
- describing what a company makes or provides
- comparing products and services

TALKING POINT

What does your company make?
What service does your company provide?
With a partner make a list.

Part A — Explaining what a company does

1 Language focus

Look at these company names. Do they make products or provide services?
What products do they make? What services do they provide?
With a partner, talk about each company.

Example: *Pepsi makes soft drinks.*

Useful language

Verbs: provide   make   be
Nouns: electronic equipment
accommodations   fast food
cars   flights   soft drinks
banking services
an internet browser
an airline
a fast food chain

PEPSI   **Panasonic**   **BURGER KING**   **citibank**   **Netscape**   **virgin atlantic**

2 Listening

Listen to Mee-Sun Yang of *Xerox* and Harvey Gill of *mbanx Direct* talking about their products and services. Choose verbs from the list below to complete the dialogs.

is	has	can

The Xerox XC-1875 .... a black and white photocopier. It .... make 18 copies per minute and .... a 700 sheet paper capacity. It .... reduce copy size down to 64% or .... enlarge up to 156%. The basic model costs $2799.

 mbanx Direct .... Canada's first direct bank. You .... do your everyday banking transactions 24 hours a day, 365 days a year through your personal computer, telephone and ATM*. With mbanx Direct, you .... speak to someone, no matter what time it is. mbanx on-line .... account information, money transfer and other services available to account holders.
Please call 800 555 1111.   *ATM – Automated Teller Machine

3 | Communication activity

STUDENT A: Look at the information on page 77.
STUDENT B: Look at the information below.

a Describe the Sharp AR 200 photocopier to Student A. Use the phrases below to help you.

It is ...
It has ...
It can ...
You can ...
It costs ...

- Digital black and white copies (b/w)
- 20 pages per minute (ppm)
- 250 sheet paper tray
- $1999

b Listen to Student A describing the Hewlett Packard Office Jet Pro 1170Cxi Multifunction.

Fill in the missing information.
Functions: copier, ... , scanner and ....
Type: digital .... copies
Speed: b/w .... ppm,
Color: .... ppm
Capacity: .... sheet paper tray
Price: $ ....

c Describe Citibank's CitiDirect Internet Banking Service to Student A.

- no registration fees
- 24 hour a day PC banking
- available in English or Japanese
- buy and sell 13 foreign currencies on-line

d Listen to Student A describing the Bank of Scotland's Offshore Account.
Fill in the missing information.

Customers: The Offshore Service is for expatriates and .... investors only.
Access: .... hour a day telephone banking
Features: no .... on interest

4 | Writing

Choose one of the companies in 1 Language focus and write sentences about the products it makes and/or the services it provides.

....
....
....
....

1 Listening

With a partner circle the words you think complete the following statements.

1 Asian Airways flies direct to *more / fewer* cities than any other airline.

2 Seats in economy class have *less / more* space so you can relax while you fly.

3 Asian Airways offers a *smaller / better* choice of meals and drinks.

4 Does this mean we're *cheaper / more expensive* than other airlines?

Now listen to an advertisement for Asian Airways and check your answers.

2 Language focus

Look at the brochures for these two cars. Work with a partner to compare them using the adjectives below.

economical exciting practical fast expensive
boring big cheap slow attractive

Useful language

more exciting than

less exciting than

as exciting as

4Runner

Starting from: $36,664
Engine: 5VZ-FE
3.4 liter, V6, 24 valve, electronic fuel injection 183kW
Fuel capacity: 70 liters
Cargo capacity: rear seat up 1.262 m³, rear seat down 2.260 m³

Celica 2000

Starting from: $23,900
Engine: 5S-FE
2.2 liter, 16 valve, electronic fuel injection 130kW
Fuel capacity: 60 liters
Cargo capacity: 0.459 m³

Write your answers.

Example: *The 4Runner is more powerful than the Celica. The Celica 2000 is cheaper than the 4Runner.*

....

....

....

....

3 Reading

Read the information about three Bangkok hotels.
a   Work with a partner to find the hotels on the map.

Useful language

The Amari ... is better for Wendy Ho because it has ...
It is cheaper than ...
There is a pool for ...
It is nearer the shops than ...

The Amari Airport Hotel

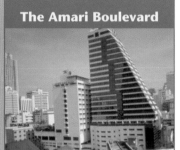

This excellent hotel is connected by air-conditioned walkway to Bangkok's international airport, making it minutes away from one of Asia's busiest hubs. Its superior accommodation, wide range of restaurants and superb business and convention facilities make it a popular choice with both business and leisure travellers.

Rooms from US $172 per night

Airport: 300m, 5 mins walk
Bangkok City Center: 25km, 25 to 40 mins by car, train or shuttle bus Future Park Shopping and Entertainment Complex: 10km, 10 mins by car

The Amari Boulevard

The Amari Boulevard Hotel is located in the heart of Bangkok's commercial and shopping district with immediate access to the airport expressway. In the immediate area of the hotel, a lively and colorful night market sells a rich variety of souvenirs, clothes and Thai handicrafts. Crib and childcare service available.

Rooms from US $140 per night

Airport: 27km, 25 to 40 mins by car
Shopping district: immediate area
Queen Sirikit Convention Center: 2km, 10 mins by car

The Amari Watergate

Minutes from the World Trade Centre and good for sightseeing, shopping and nightlife, the Amari Watergate Hotel could not have a better location. The excellent accommodations and facilities, which include a selection of fine restaurants, a business centre and a fitness centre make this hotel an exceptional choice for a Bangkok base.

Rooms from US $184 per night

Airport: 24km, 25 mins by car, train or shuttle bus
World Trade Center 500m, 25 to 40 mins walk
Queen Sirikit Convention Center - 8km, 20 mins by car

b   With your partner, compare the hotels and decide which would be best for these visitors to Bangkok. Make notes about your choices. Explain your choices to the class.

Mr. and Mrs. Bertrand Fischer Mr. and Mrs. Fischer are from Germany. They will visit Bangkok for one week on vacation. They have two children aged three and five. They want to go sightseeing and shopping.

Ms. Wendy Ho Ms. Ho is the Marketing Director of a company based in Hong Kong. She will visit Bangkok for only two days and her schedule is very busy. She will visit her company's distributors in Thailand. She is worried about getting caught in the Bangkok traffic.

Mr. Vijai Shah Mr. Shah is from India. He wants to stay in Bangkok for one week to go shopping and enjoy the restaurants and bars at night.

4 Exploring

Identify your major competitors. Compare your products and services with theirs. Fill in the information in the table.

Competitor	Product/Service

Review 1

Vocabulary 1 Prepositions

Choose five things in the classroom. Write a sentence for each. Say where it is.
Use the prepositions from the list below.

on   in   near   above   next to   behind   under   in front of

clock..............................	It's on the wall .above.. the whiteboard.
Junko's..books......................	They're on the floor.under. her chair.
1	....
2	....
3	....
4	....
5	....

Now work in pairs. Read your sentence, but don't tell your partner what the thing is.
Your partner will try to guess what it is. Then change roles.

Language 1   Introductions

a   Complete the following sentence with the correct prepositions.

in   for   of

1   This is Mr. Chan. Mr. Chan is the CEO .... Mediation Corp.
2   Those two people are Linda and Paul. Linda and Paul work .... the accounts department.
3   I work .... XYZ Ltd. XYZ is a computer company. XYZ's Head Office is .... Beijing.
4   I am a Sales representative .... Thaiway Company. The Sales representatives travel to many countries.
5   My office is .... the suburbs of Hanoi. My office is very modern.
6   My company is American. The Head Office is .... New York. I work .... the Kuala Lumpur office. My office is very busy.

b   In English we do not often repeat nouns. Look at the sentences again. Which nouns can you change to a pronoun?

Example: This is Mr. Chan. ~~Mr Chan~~ He is the CEO of Mediation Corp.

I/my   you/your   he/his   she/her   it/its   we/our   they/their

Communication 1

Work in pairs to introduce yourselves.

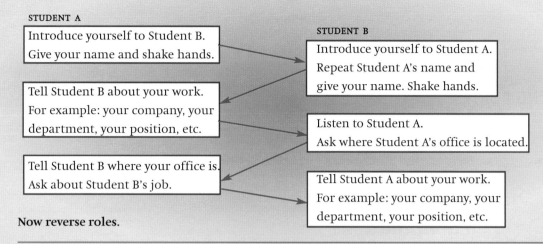

STUDENT A

Introduce yourself to Student B.
Give your name and shake hands.

Tell Student B about your work.
For example: your company, your
department, your position, etc.

Tell Student B where your office is.
Ask about Student B's job.

STUDENT B

Introduce yourself to Student A.
Repeat Student A's name and
give your name. Shake hands.

Listen to Student A.
Ask where Student A's office is located.

Tell Student A about your work.
For example: your company, your
department, your position, etc.

Now reverse roles.

Vocabulary 2   Adjectives

a   Look at these two lists of adjectives.
Draw a line between the antonyms (opposites).

A	B
1 uneconomical	a small
2 big	b convenient
3 cheap	c exciting
4 slow	d expensive
5 inconvenient	e economical
6 attractive	f ugly
7 boring	g fast
8 safe	h dangerous

b   Now think of five products or services.
Choose positive adjectives from list B to
describe them.

Product/Service	Positive adjectives
walkman	small

Language 2   Comparisons

Use the adjectives above to complete these sentences.

Example: A walkman is smaller than a home music system.

An ATM is more convenient than standing in line in a bank.

1   Tokyo ....
2   Flying ....
3   The Hilton Hotel ....
4   A credit card ....
5   My office ....
6   The internet ....

Communication 2

**Work in pairs. Your company/university/school is thinking about moving locations.
Think of a new location anywhere in your country. Decide which location is better.
Give reasons for your decision by comparing the two locations.**

Time zones

UNIT GOALS
- telling the time
- schedules

TALKING POINT

What time do you start work?

What time is it now?

What time is it now in New York?

What time do you have lunch?

What time do you go home?

| Part A | Telling the time |

1 Language focus

Match these times to the email messages below.

1 Twenty after six **D**   2 Quarter to nine ☐   3 Noon ☐

4 Ten to ten ☐   5 Two o'clock ☐   6 Half past six ☐

A Date: Fri, 30 Jun 2000 20:45:51 +0900
X-Sender: mami@fastnet.or.jp

B Date: Wed, 11 Nov 2000 14:00:28 +0100
X-Sender: florence@normandie.net.fr

C Date: Sun, 23 Dec 2000 09:50:12 -0500
X-Sender: justin@nyc.com

D Date: Mon, 30 Jul 2000 18:20:04 +0700
X-Sender: sugunya@siamnet.co.th

E Date: Fri, 06 Aug 2000 06:30:27 +1000
X-Sender: Thomas@surfcity.co.au

F Date: Sat, 21 Feb 2000 12:00:03 -0800
X-Sender: schultz@lawide.com

2 Communication activity

STUDENT A: **Figure out what time it was in your country when the email messages A to C above were sent. Use the Time zones map in the Help folder if you need to. Give the answers to Student B.**

STUDENT B: **Figure out what time it was in your country when the email messages D to F above were sent. Use the Time zones map in the Help folder if you need to. Give the answers to Student A.**

Email	Time in your country
A	
B	
C	

Email	Time in your country
D	
E	
F	

3 Culture focus

Ken Murphy is a company manager living in Chicago. Read about his typical work week. How does his work week compare to yours?

> I always try to get to the office early because I work better in the mornings. I usually arrive at 7:30. I take a late lunch at 1:30 because the restaurants are less crowded then. I leave my office around 5:00 so I can spend some time with my kids before they go to bed. I never work on weekends.

Lunch time

1 When do most people take lunch in your country?
2 Does your company decide when you have lunch?
3 How long do people take for lunch?

Leave work

1 What time do you leave your office in the evening?
2 Is working late common in your country?
3 Do you work on weekends?

4 Listening

Listen to people from around the world talking about their work day. Fill in the missing information.

Michael Devas, New York
Starts work: ..9:30am..............
Lunch: ....
Leaves work: ...7:30pm.............
Weekend: ....

Marcel Marquez, Madrid, Spain
Starts work:............................
Lunch: ..2:00–5:00pm...............
Leaves work:...........................
Weekend: ...Sundays..................

Sharon Davies, Los Angeles
Starts work: ....
Lunch: ....
Leaves work: ..6:00pm.............
Weekend: ....

Julie Edwards, Florida
Starts work:..8:00am................
Lunch: ....
Leaves work:.5:30pm.................
Weekend: ....

5 Communication activity

STUDENT A: Look at the information on page 77.
STUDENT B: Look at the information below.

STUDENT B: In your local time, when is the best time to call:
a Julie Edwards
b Sharon Davies?

e.g. **Example A:** When's the best time to call Michael Devas in New York? B: Well, you can call him between (time) and (time) but don't call him (say when).

Now ask Student A when the best time is to call:
a Michael Devas
b Marcel Marquez.

Compare your answers with a partner.

1 Reading

An American business woman, Wendy Smith, is coming to visit your company in Taipei. Read the email message she sent.
Check ☑ the things below she wants you to do for her.

```
                    ▭ Fixing schedules
  Send Now   Send Later   📄  📎  ✍ Signature ▼  Options ▼    ▦

  Date: Mon, 11 May 2000 21:39:31 - 1700
  To: you@yourcompany.com
  From: wsmith@gaol.com
  Subject: The Taiwan trade fair

  Dear … ,

  Thank you for offering to arrange my schedule during the trade fair.
  Following are several requests:
  My flight arrives Friday October 15th at 16:40, (Flight number UA 868).
  Please arrange for someone to meet me at the airport. Could you also please
  book a hotel for me for three nights: I return to the US on the 10:30 flight
  (Flight number UA 867) on Monday the 18th.
  At the fair I'd like to make a two-hour presentation and give a one-hour
  demonstration. Could you arrange them for me? I'd also like to have dinner
  with you and your colleagues as you suggested. I'd love to eat Chinese.
  Could you find a time that's best for everyone and make a reservation at a
  good restaurant?
  Finally, I hope to have a little free time for sightseeing and shopping. I'd
  be really grateful if you could suggest some places to visit.
  Thanks very much for all your help. Looking forward to receiving my
  schedule and meeting you all.

  Best regards

  Wendy
```

hotel reservation ☐
go sightseeing ☐
arrange the schedule ☐
give a presentation ☐
arrange a meeting ☐
make a reservation
  at a restaurant ☐
go shopping ☐
meet her at the airport ☐
book flights ☐
email her ☐

2 Vocabulary

Read the email message in **1 Reading** again. Find the verbs to match the nouns below.

1 .... my schedule.
2 My flight ....
3 .... me at the airport .
4 ....a presentation.

5 .... demonstration.
6 .... dinner.
7 .... a reservation.
8 .... some places to visit.

3 Communication activity

Work in pairs. Plan Wendy Smith's schedule for her. Write the times and the activities in the planner.

Quick Guide

The Grand Hotel – Taipei

A luxury hotel overlooking the city of Taipei. Great location and excellent service. Superb restaurants await you. English speaking staff throughout the hotel. Make your trip to Taipei one to remember.

→ Visit the night markets at Dinghao

The Grand Hotel Notice to Guests
Breakfast will be served in the main dining hall from 07:00 to 09:30 daily.

Trade Fair Main Hall

Over 150 exhibitors have booths with large displays and demonstrations. The exhibition will be open on Sat /Sun from 10:00 to 17:00. Lunch available.

Special tours for Trade Fair participants

You will be taken by bus for a tour of the city to see famous temples and gardens. Each tour takes approximately four hours.

Tours leave from the hotel on both days at the following times: 9:00 13:00 17:00

National Palace Museum

Art from 5,000 years of China's history. Open daily from 10:00 to 18:00.

Dinghao

All types of restaurants, cuisines, department stores and boutiques, movie theatres, bakeries, book shops, art galleries, and more! Some good deals on clothes and souvenirs in the area's maze of alleys.

Arrange to meet Wendy at the airport and take her to her hotel (tell her the name of the hotel). Decide where to go shopping and sightseeing. Choose a restaurant to go to for dinner. Plan all the activities she wants to do.

Useful language

I think she should give a presentation at 11:00.

What do you think?

I agree.

Um ... I'm not sure.

I think she should ...

Schedule: FRIDAY	
Time	Activity
17:00	Pick up from airport
17:30	Check in at The Grand Hotel
20:30	....

Schedule: SUNDAY	
Time	Activity
....	....
....	....
....	....

Schedule: SATURDAY	
Time	Activity
8:30	Have breakfast at hotel
....	....
....	....

Schedule: MONDAY	
Time	Activity
8:00	Check out of hotel
....	....
....	....

Explain your schedule to another pair. How is your schedule different?

---

4   Writing

Work in pairs. Write an email to Wendy explaining her schedule to her. Show your email to another pair when you have finished.

<table>
<tr><td></td><td></td><td></td></tr>
</table>

UNIT 5	# On the phone

UNIT GOALS
- requesting information
- checking spelling
- telephone phrases

TALKING POINT

At work, how many of these things do you do on the telephone in English? How many things do your colleagues do? Check ☑ the boxes.

		You	Your colleagues
1	make business calls	☐	☐
2	receive business calls	☐	☐
3	make appointments	☐	☐
4	place orders	☐	☐
5	receive orders	☐	☐

Part A   Answering the phone

1 Language focus

Work with a partner. Read the three telephone conversation extracts. Fill in the blanks using the words or phrases from the box.

Speaking   Just a moment please   My name is   Who should I say is calling   How can I help you
Do you speak English   I'll put you through   Can I help you   Can I speak to   Could you repeat that please

1   A: Hello, Mitchell Designs.
    B: .... Ms. Sampson please?
    A: ....
    B: Ah. Hello. My name is Peter Rogers of ...

2   A: East Asia Credit Bank. .... ?
    B: Hello. Ms. Pitsamai Keree's office please.
    A: .... ?
    B: Julianne Hunter.
    A: Just a moment. ....

3   A: *Kansai Rayon de gozaimasu.*
    B: Uh ... hello ... . ?
    A: Yes, a little.
    B: .... Mel Douglas of Trenchard Carpets. Can I speak with Mr. Jyoji Matsuo please?
    A: ....

Listen to the three telephone conversations to check your answers.

2 Communication activity

STUDENT A: Look at the information on page 78. Role play the situations.
STUDENT B: Look at the information below. Role play the situations.

Situation 1

You are Ms. Holly Kronfeld of the Far East Research Institute. Call the University of Michigan and ask to speak to Professor Harold Buchowski.

Situation 2

You are Mr. Hideo Takanashi of Yamanaka Industries. Take a call. Make a note of who called you.

Situation 3

You are Mr. Victor Stoltz from the government tax office. Call Chock-a-Block Toys Ltd, and ask to speak to Mr. Eric Lum.

Situation 4

You are Ms. Li-An Kim of the International Bank of Shanghai. You are in the office with two other people, Mr. David Barber and Ms. An-Li Wang. Take a call. Answer in your own language at first. Make a note of who called you.

---

3 Culture focus

Read the article. Then answer the questions. 2 min

If the cell phone had a cord, you could almost strangle the user

During a recent performance of *Death of a Salesman*, its star, Brian Dennehy, was startled to hear a cell phone ring near the end of the second act. Even more disturbing was to hear the phone being answered and a woman in the audience clearly saying, 'It's almost finished,' and going on to make dinner plans.

1 Do you have a cell phone?
2 What do you think of this woman's behavior?
3 In groups, make a set of guidelines for when it is *not* okay to use a cell phone. 3-4 min

Example: You shouldn't use your cell phone in the cinema. Complete sentences

....

....

....

....

....

1   Brainstorming

In small groups, brainstorm a list of questions for Mai and Wajan to ask. Use the questions in the box below to help you.

a

Mai Kurihara is calling Jupiter Printing Company. She wants to get a price list for this year. She wants to receive the prices by fax.

b

Wajan Sukcharoen of Jupiter Printing Company receives a call from Mai Kurihara who wants to get a price list for this year.

List of questions
Can you ...?
Could you ...?
Can I have your ...?

2   Communication activity

STUDENT A: Look at the information on page 78.
STUDENT B: Look at the information below.

Situation 1
You are Mr. Jun Takahashi of Industrial Air Conditioning. A customer calls. Fill in the form.

Situation 2
You are Mai Kurihara. Call Jupiter Printing Company and ask them to fax you a price list for this year.

Customer request form

Request for

	office	factory
air conditioner brochures	☐	☐
air conditioner price information	☐	☐
installation information	☐	☐

Name: ....

Address: ....

Tel: ....

Fax: ....

Email: ....

Notes: ....

MARKETING SERVICES JAPAN

MAI KURIHARA

SALES MANAGER

3-20-15 Shin Osaka, Osaka fu, Japan
Tel: (06) 8644 3976 Fax: (06) 8644 3900
Email: kurihara-m@msj.co.jp

3 Listening

a Listen to two telephone conversations. Fill in the forms with the necessary information.

1

Name: ....

Company: ....

Fax:...

Request: ☐ print brochure ☐ price list ☐ visit
         ☐ quotation ☐ other (specify)

Notes *send immediately*...................................

2

Name: ....

Address: *Heiwa Life Insurance, 2–5–15 Ogikubo, Suginami-ku, Tokyo.*

Request: ☐ office A/C brochure ☐ price list
         ☐ factory A/C brochure ☐ visit
         ☐ other (specify)

Notes ....

---

b Listen again. Finish the questions asked in each conversation.

1 Can you send me .... by .... please?
2 Could I have your .... and .... please?
3 .... spell .... please?
4 Could you send me .... for .... please?
5 Can I have your .... and .... please?

c With a partner, compare the questions asked in the two conversations.
1 Are they similar to the ones you made in **1 Brainstorming**?
2 Were your conversations in **2 Communication activity** similar to or different from the ones on the tape? For example, were they longer/shorter, more polite, etc.?

---

4 Communication activity

With a partner, practice making and receiving calls. Take turns asking for information and getting customer details. Use the information below. Follow the conversation pattern.

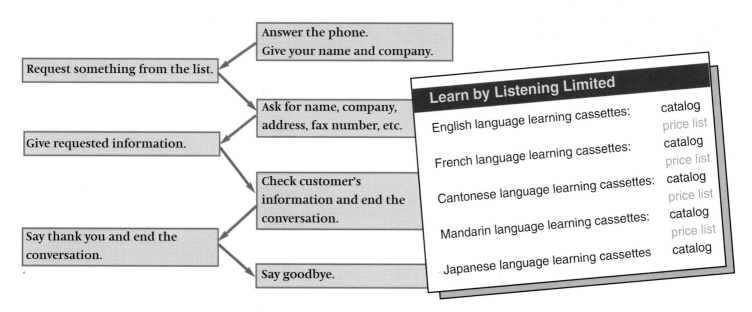

Answer the phone.
Give your name and company.

Request something from the list.

Ask for name, company, address, fax number, etc.

Give requested information.

Check customer's information and end the conversation.

Say thank you and end the conversation.

Say goodbye.

Learn by Listening Limited

English language learning cassettes: catalog price list

French language learning cassettes: catalog price list

Cantonese language learning cassettes: catalog price list

Mandarin language learning cassettes: catalog price list

Japanese language learning cassettes catalog

UNIT 6

Placing an order

UNIT GOALS
- ordering and complaining
- some / many / a few
- countable and uncountable nouns

TALKING POINT

How do you order these things in your company? Put checks ☑ in the table.

Item	Talk to my boss	Ask the Purchasing Manager	Order myself	Other
pens and pencils paper furniture computer software electrical equipment				

Compare with your classmates.

Part A — Ordering what you need

1 Listening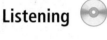

a Kay Johnson is in charge of buying clothing at her pharmaceutical company. Listen to her talking to two colleagues, Sung-Ho and Ron. How many of each item do they need?

Kay Johnson
Purchasing Manager

Sung-Ho Choi
Engineering Manager

Ron Irvine
Maintenance Supervisor

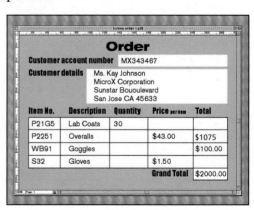

b Now listen to Kay call her supplier with the complete order. Fill in the missing information on the computer screen.
1 How many goggles did she order?
2 How much do they cost?

Check your answers with a partner.

WORKWEAR

Gloves S32

Overalls P2251

Goggles WB91

Order by phone or fax Lab coats P21G5

Order

Customer account number MX343467

Customer details Ms. Kay Johnson
MicroX Corporation
Sunstar Bououlevard
San Jose CA 45633

Item No.	Description	Quantity	Price per item	Total
P21G5	Lab Coats	30		
P2251	Overalls		$43.00	$1075
WB91	Goggles			$100.00
S32	Gloves		$1.50	
			Grand Total	$2000.00

2 Brainstorming

In small groups, brainstorm a list of things that you buy in your office.
Put the words into the table.

Some things cannot be put in the
shaded parts of the table.
Do you know why?
Look in the Help folder on page 89.
if you don't know.

a lot of	
many	
some	
a few	
just a few / not many	
not a lot of	

3 Communication activity

Work in small groups. You are opening a new sales office for
your company. There will be ten employees including yourselves.
Decide what you need in the office.

We need ten chairs.
We need a carpet.
We don't need a photocopier.
We only need one telephone.
We need some plants.
Now find a partner from a different group and ask each other
about your offices. What do you need? How many/much do
you need?

4 Culture focus

Look at the photographs and answer the questions below.

1 Where would you expect to find people dressed like this?
2 What is the dress code in your office/company/college/country?
3 Do you have a uniform?

1   Brainstorming

What can go wrong with an order? Look at the examples below. With a partner, continue the list.

wrong price per item, wrong address, wrong quantity

....

....

2   Listening 💿

ESL

Electric Supplies Limited, 44 Bukit Batok Close, #01–23, Singapore 456344
Tel 65 4559 875 Fax 65 4559 843 Email customerservice@esl.com.sg

INVOICE

Customer
Supersaver Supermarkets
55-66 Sembawang Terrace
Singapore 312456

Contact
Ms.P Xiang

Item	Description	Quantity	Price/item	Total
C90XD	C90 cassette tape	50	2.00	100.00
DX9-120	120 min digital video	20	16.30	326.00
L100WS	100W light bulb	20	0.99	19.80
FL120S	120cm fluorescent light	20	2.24	44.80
			Sub Total	490.60
			Discount	24.53
			Tax (10%)	46.60
Please pay this invoice within 30 days			Grand Total	512.67

a   Paula Xiang from Supersaver Supermarkets has received this invoice. She is not happy with it so she calls Electric Supplies. Listen to the conversation and answer the questions.

1   What two things are wrong with the invoice?
2   Does the supplier:
    a complain b laugh c apologize d do nothing?

b   Listen again. What action does the supplier take? Choose an answer from the Action list.

1   Problem 1 ....
2   Problem 2 ....

Action
a   I'll give you a 5% discount.
b   I'll confirm that with the salesperson and send you a new invoice.
c   I'll send you ten more light strips.
d   Put them all back on the truck.
e   Put ten back on the truck.

3 Language focus

STUDENT A: Look at the information on page 79.
STUDENT B: Look at the information below.

Student A should choose a complaint from his/her list. You should choose an apology and action from your list below. Student A will then choose a follow-up. Take turns.

Example: **Complaint** I was promised a 10% discount, but I only got 5.
Apology I'm sorry about that. **Action** I'll check with the salesperson and send you a revised invoice.

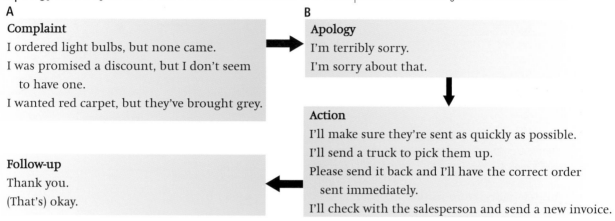

A

Complaint
I ordered light bulbs, but none came.
I was promised a discount, but I don't seem
    to have one.
I wanted red carpet, but they've brought grey.

Follow-up
Thank you.
(That's) okay.

B

Apology
I'm terribly sorry.
I'm sorry about that.

Action
I'll make sure they're sent as quickly as possible.
I'll send a truck to pick them up.
Please send it back and I'll have the correct order
    sent immediately.
I'll check with the salesperson and send a new invoice.

4 Communication activity

STUDENT A: Look at the information on page 79.
STUDENT B: Look at the information below.

Situation 1
Look at the computer catalog and the invoice you received from Student A for the order you placed. Find the mistake, then call Student A and complain.

COMPUTER WORLD
INCREASE YOUR MEMORY

Rewritable CD Drive	$450.00
Superdisk Drive	$280.00
MO Drive (230MB)	$210.00
Zip Drive	$199.00
Rewritable 600MB CDs (5 pack)	$55.00
Superdisk (3 Pack)	$28.95
MO Disk (230MB)each	$ 7.55
Zip Disk (10 Pack)	$95.95

Invoice

1 X Zip Drive XC250AM	$280.00
Zip disk (10 pack) R2200X	$ 95.95
	$375.95

Situation 2
Look at the order form you received from Student A and the invoice you sent. Student A will call to complain about a mistake on your invoice. Apologize and offer to take some action.

ORDER	
	12 x desk AM25P
	1 x executive desk AM40E
	12 x swivel chairs PJ25P
	1 x executive chair Pz90E

INVOICE		
12 x desk AM25P	$292.00ea	$3504.00
1 x executive desk AM40E	$628.00ea	$ 628.00
20 x swivel chairs PJ25P	$ 62.90ea	$1258.00
1 x executive chair Pz90E	$252.80ea	$ 252.80
		$5642.80

Review 2

Vocabulary 1

a Match the times to the clocks.

1 seven fifty-five
2 nine thirty
3 twenty past two
4 quarter after four
5 three o'clock
6 five after ten

b If these are the times in your country, what are the times in New Zealand?
   (Use the Time zones map in the Help folder for Unit 4.) Tell your partner your answers.

Language 1

Put this telephone conversation in order.

a I'm just putting you through, Ms. Simpson.   ☐
b Just a moment please. Who should I say is calling?   ☐
c Linda Simpson of Samsung, UK.   ☐
d Hello, Bradley's. Can I help you?   ☐
e Can I speak to Felix Mendez please?   ☐

Communication 1

a Plan a one-day schedule for a colleague visiting from an overseas office. You must include meetings with the company chairperson, yourself and a visit to a factory. Include anything else you think is necessary.

b Now in pairs, call each other and give details of the schedule. Write down the schedule your partner has prepared for you.

9.00	
10.00	
11.00	
12.00	
13.00	
14.00	
15.00	
16.00	
17.00	
18.00	
19.00	
20.00	

9.00	
10.00	
11.00	
12.00	
13.00	
14.00	
15.00	
16.00	
17.00	
18.00	
19.00	
20.00	

Vocabulary 2

Which of these words can be used with *how many* and which with *how much*? Put a check ✔ for each one.

	how many...?	how much...?
desks		
staff		
things		
stuff		
computers		
problems		
solutions		
trouble		
cash		

Which of the words can be used with *a lot of*?

Language 2

Look at the apology below. How many words can you think of to put in the blanks?

I'm ..*terribly*. sorry about that.

....

Communication 2

Look at the brochures here. In pairs, practice calling each other to place orders. When you are taking the order, make sure you give the final price to the caller.

Making a reservation

UNIT GOALS
- making a reservation at a hotel
- reserving an airline ticket
- renting a car
- want to …, would like to…

TALKING POINT

Do you do these things for your work? Check ☑ the boxes.

stay in hotels ☐   rent a car ☐   go to restaurants ☐   travel by airplane ☐

Part A   Booking a service

1   Brainstorming

Look at the hotel receptionist's computer screen. Alex Meyer wants to book a room.
With a partner, brainstorm the questions he might hear.

Write your questions here.

Example: *May I have your name please?*

....

....

....

....

....

2   Language focus

Put the words below in the correct order to make the questions the receptionist asked Alex. Compare the
questions with the ones you made in 1 Brainstorming.

1   name / May / I / please / your / have ? ....

2   staying / When / will / be / you ?..

3   Can / telephone / your / number / have / I ?..

4   spell / Could / you / that / please ?..

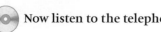 Now listen to the telephone conversation and check your answers.

3 Listening

a Listen to Lucy Zhang making an airline reservation. Fill in the form.

b Listen again. Fill in the missing words below. Check your answers with a partner.

Booking Form

Name :	Lucy Zhang		
Date	...........March	time	.............am
from	....	to	....
Flight #	CHA901		

AGENT: First Travel. James speaking. Can I help you?

LUCY: Uh ... . reserve a flight one-way to Tokyo please.

AGENT: When will you be flying, ma'am?

LUCY: Tomorrow. March 4th.

AGENT: There is a flight with North East Airways on the 4th leaving Los Angeles at 11:05 am.

LUCY: Mmm ... .

AGENT: Can I have your name please?

LUCY: Lucy Zhang.

AGENT: Could you spell your last name please?

LUCY: .... It's Z – H – A – N – G.

AGENT: How will you be paying, Ms. Zhang?

LUCY: By credit card. The number is 4535 1567 3765 4354.

AGENT: OK, Ms. Zhang. Can I confirm your booking? You will be flying with North East Airways to Tokyo leaving Los Angeles tomorrow at 11:05. Please pick up your ticket from the check-in counter. Please remember to check in two hours before the flight time.

LUCY: ....

4 Communication activity

STUDENT A: Look at the information on page 80. Role-play the situations.

STUDENT B: Look at the information below. Role-play the situations.

Situation 1

You are the receptionist at the Park Hotel. Student A will call you. Take his or her reservation. Use the screen in 1 Brainstorming to help you ask the right questions.

Situation 2

You want to fly to Seoul next Saturday, returning one week later. Call Student A at *First Travel* and make a reservation.

1   Brainstorming

You are in the United States and need to rent a car. You have to drive long distances, so you need a comfortable car that doesn't use too much gasoline. You'd also like to use the car to take clients to business lunches. Look at these cars. With a partner, decide which one is most suitable for your business needs.

Useful language

I think A is best because ...

I agree / disagree ...

B is better because it is / it has ...

comfortable   spacious   fast   economic   stylish

---

2   Listening

a   Listen to Angel Tan reserve a rental car for when she arrives at JFK airport. Answer these questions.

1   When will she be arriving in the United States?
   a 5/22   *b* 4/22   *c* 5/25   *d* 4/25

4   What is her fax number?
   a Singapore 256 2398   *b Bangalore 256 3298*
   c Singapore 256 3298

2   How many days does she want the car?
   a 2   b 3   c 4   d 1

5   Which car did she choose?

3   What size car does she want?
   a compact   b sedan   c mini van

b   Look at the photos again. Which car would you choose? Why?

3 Communication activity

Work in pairs to make reservations.

1 Choose one of the following services.

| Hotel | Airline ticket agency | Car rental agency |

You will take reservations for your service.

2 Make a form to fill in for taking reservations for your choice of service. Use the sample form here to help you.

3 Make a sign for your service.

4 One student should stay at the desk taking reservations. The other should move around the classroom making reservations for a hotel, a flight and a car. Go to as many agencies as possible.

Choose the services you think are best. Take notes. When you are finished, change roles. You can also use the vocabulary in the Help folder on page 90 to help you.

Sample form

(NAME OF AGENCY)..

NAME ....

DATE ....

OTHER DETAIL ....

DATE OF TRAVEL / CHECK IN.....................................

RETURN DATE / CHECK OUT.......................................

TOTAL COST ....

TEL NUMBER ....

BOOKING REFERENCE...

Useful language

Vocabulary

Hotel
When ...?   How many ...?   single or double occupancy/room
telephone number

Airline ticket agency
When ...?   Where ...?   one way   round trip
telephone number

Car rental agency
When ...?   How many ...?   time   compact, mid-size, full size
telephone number

4 Reporting

Work with a partner. Use your notes and the words below to tell the class which services you chose.

We chose .... because ....

| cheaper   efficient   better value for money   helpful   choice   suited my needs   good service |

5 Culture focus

In the US the date is written 3/25/02. It is said 'March 25th 2002'. In the UK the same date is written 25/3/02 and is said 'the 25th of March 2002' or 'March the 25th, 2002'.

How do you write and say the date in your country? Is it the same as the US or the UK? Or different from both?

UNIT 8

Getting around

UNIT GOALS   • getting around town
                • arriving at an appointment

TALKING POINT

How do you get to work?   By bus / car / train / bike / on foot?

How easy is it for visitors to find your office?   Easy / Not too difficult / difficult

What department do you work in?   Sales   Administration   Production   Other

Part A   Getting around town

1   Reading

Read the email and find Kumiko's office building on the map.

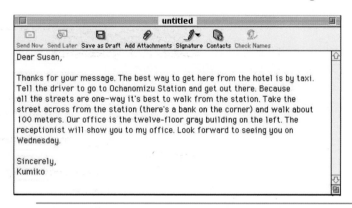

Dear Susan,

Thanks for your message. The best way to get here from the hotel is by taxi. Tell the driver to go to Ochanomizu Station and get out there. Because all the streets are one-way it's best to walk from the station. Take the street across from the station (there's a bank on the corner) and walk about 100 meters. Our office is the twelve-floor gray building on the left. The receptionist will show you to my office. Look forward to seeing you on Wednesday.

Sincerely,
Kumiko

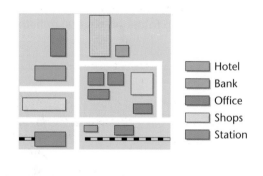

- Hotel
- Bank
- Office
- Shops
- Station

Compare your answer with a partner.

2   Language focus

Work in pairs. Use the verbs below to complete the dialogs. You don't need to use them all.

start	get on	come	finish	stop	change	get off	go	take	go to

1   WOMAN: Excuse me.

     CLERK: Yes.

     WOMAN: I want to .... Silom Road.

     CLERK: Go to the right platform. ....
the first train .... at Siam to the
train for Saphan Taksin. .... at
Sala Dang station which is on the Silom Road.

     WOMAN: Thank you. How many stations from Siam?

     CLERK: It's the second station.

     WOMAN: Thank you very much.

     CLERK: You're welcome.

2   MAN: Excuse me.

     CLERK: Can I help you?

     MAN: How do I get to Suidobashi?

     CLERK: .... any train from platform 1.
.... at Ochanomizu.
.... the local train – it's yellow.
.... at the next station.
That's it.

     MAN: Thank you.

     CLERK: No problem.

3 Listening

Listen to three conversations. In each conversation a business person is asking how to get to the next appointment. Fill in the blanks for each conversation.

| walk | take a bus | take a taxi | take a train | go | turn | change | get on | get off |

1 .... to the end of the street and .... left. .... straight until you reach the station. .... from platform 1 and .... at Tokyo station. .... the Marunouchi line one stop to Ginza. Ask someone for the building when you get there.

2 .... from outside and tell the driver to take you to the Landmark Hotel. .... out of the hotel and .... left. .... along the street and the office you want is the second building on the right.

3 .... across the road to the station. .... to Shibuya and .... there. .... outside the station and .... to the office. The driver can take you right to the door.

4 Communication activity

STUDENT A: Look at the information on page 80.
STUDENT B: Look at the information below.

You are a clerk at Akasaka station in Fukuoka. Student A is a visitor to Fukuoka. Answer his or her questions.

Now you are a visitor to Beijing. Student A is a clerk at Qianmen station. Ask Student A how to get to these places.

| **Drum Tower** | **Wanshow Rd** | **Dongzhimen** |

Make notes.

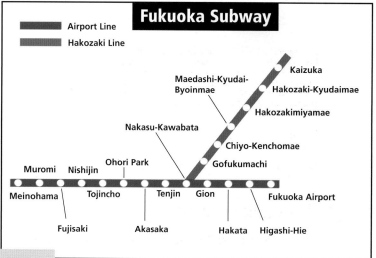

Akasaka Station
Platform 1 – to Fukuoka Airport
Platform 2 – to Meinohama

5 Exploring

Work with a partner. Give instructions on how to get to your office from the main station.

Useful language

Exit the station.
Turn right/left.
Take the second left/right.
It's the third building on the right.
It's across from/next to/near ...

1   Brainstorming

Look at this picture of a company's reception desk.
Work with a partner to label the things you see.

1   How is it similar or different from your company's reception area?
2   What do you think the people are saying?

Receptionist: ....

Visitor: ....

2   Listening

Listen to two people arriving at a company's reception. Check ☑ the things they talk about.

	Conversation 1	Conversation 2
Their own name	✔	
The name of the person they want to see		
Appointment		
Department name		

3   Language focus

There are two conversations mixed up here. Conversation1/Conversation 2 is between a visitor and the receptionist. The second is between the visitor and the person he has come to see. Put them in order.

	Conversation 1	Conversation 2
1 Thank you for seeing me today.	Good morning. Can I help you?	Hello. I'm Richard Chandler.
2 Thank you. Here's mine.	....	....
3 Hello my name is John Grafton and I'm here to see Mr. Chandler in Accounts.	.... Just a moment please.	.... Nice to meet you too.
4 Hello. I'm Richard Chandler.	....	....
5 Nice to meet you.	....	....
6 Not at all.	....	....
7 Good morning. Can I help you?	....	.·...
8 Just a moment please.	....	....
9 Nice to meet you too.	....	....
10 Hello. I'm John Grafton.	....	....
11 He'll be down in a moment.	....	....
12 Please take a seat.	....	....
13 Thank you.	....	....
14 Here's my business card.	....	....

4 Culture focus

Are there rules for giving and receiving business cards in
your country? What do you know about other countries?
Do people shake hands in your country? Are there rules
for shaking hands? How close should you stand to someone
when you talk to them?

5 Communication activity

STUDENT A: **You are the receptionist.**
STUDENT B: **You are a visitor. You want to see John Baker in Sales.**

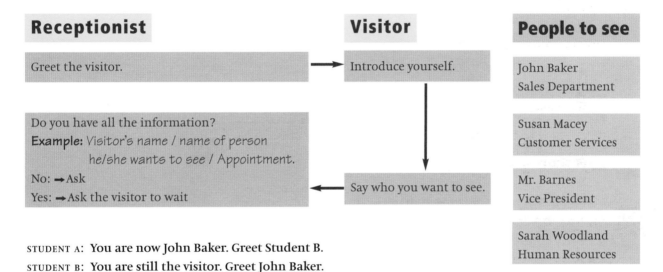

Receptionist

Greet the visitor.

Do you have all the information?
Example: Visitor's name / name of person
he/she wants to see / Appointment.
No: →Ask
Yes: →Ask the visitor to wait

Visitor

Introduce yourself.

Say who you want to see.

People to see

John Baker
Sales Department

Susan Macey
Customer Services

Mr. Barnes
Vice President

Sarah Woodland
Human Resources

STUDENT A: **You are now John Baker. Greet Student B.**
STUDENT B: **You are still the visitor. Greet John Baker.**

John Baker

Greet the visitor.

Offer your business card.

Say thank you. Offer the visitor
a seat or offer to take him/her
to your office.

Visitor

Greet John Baker.
Shake hands.

Say thank you.
Offer your business card.

Now reverse roles.
STUDENT B: **You are the receptionist .**
STUDENT A: **You are a visitor. You want to see Susan Macey in Customer Services.**

About the company

UNIT GOALS
- talking about the company history
- reporting on company changes

TALKING POINT

When did your company start?

What are some of the important events in your company's history?

What has changed recently in your company?

Part A Talking about company history

1 Listening

a   Change the verbs into the past tense form.

	past tense
1 launch	
2 sell	
3 meet	
4 develop	
5 make	

b   Listen to a history of Apple Computer. Number the pictures in order as you hear them.

Apple I

imac

Steve Jobs

1984

April 1st, 1976

c   Listen again. Put one verb under each picture.

2 Writing

Work in pairs. Use the verbs to tell the Apple Computer story in your own words. Compare your writing with another pair.

3 Brainstorming

What do you know about your company's history? Work in pairs to write notes. Use the verbs below to help you.

began developed sold made built changed opened

Example: .... began to sell or began selling ....

....

....

....

....

....

4 Reporting

Prepare a presentation about the history of your company or a company that interests you. Use your ideas from 3 Brainstorming.

- What is the company name?
- What kind of company is it? What products or services does it have?
- Who started the company?
- What was the company like at the beginning?
- What was its first success?
- What was its biggest failure? e.g. a new product that didn't sell
- How is the company today?

Present your company to the rest of the class.

Useful language

What happened *after that*? What happened *next*?
What happened *then*? Do you know what happened *next*?

Part B   Company changes

1   Vocabulary

Match the verbs on the left with their opposites on the right.

1	increase	a	stay
2	move	b	decrease
3	build	c	reduce
4	join	d	remove
5	expand	e	leave
6	change	f	remain the same

2   Language focus

The past tense must be used if the sentence has a past time reference.
The present perfect can be used if there is no past time reference.

Past time references:	
Yesterday	In 1999
Last week	Last month
Ten years ago	Two months ago

Examples:

The company *moved* its office from Penang to Kuala Lumpur ten years ago. *(ten years ago = past tense)*
The company *has moved* its office from Penang to Kuala Lumpur. *(no time reference = present perfect)*

Jane Walters and Sam Riches *left* the company last week. *(last week = past tense)*
Jane Walters and Sam Riches *have left* the company. *(no time reference = present perfect)*

Work with a partner to complete the sentences below. Decide if you need
the Past tense or Present perfect tense. Look at the Help folder on page 92
to help you.

1   How were the sales figures last month?
     They .... *(increase)* by 7%.

2   Have you got any new staff?
     Yes we have. Two new accountants .... *(join)* the company.

3   Have you expanded production?
     Yes. We .... *(build)* a new factory in 1999.

4   Have you entered the Chinese market yet?
     Yes. We .... *(open)* a new showroom in Shanghai.

5   This office seems bigger. Have you expanded it?
     Yes. The company .... *(expand)* it office space last summer.

6   Is your product range the same as last year?
     No. We .... *(reduce)* the number of products we offer.

3 Communication activity

STUDENT A: Look at the information on page 81.
STUDENT B: Look at the information below.

Student A has just returned from a visit to E&P Co. Ltd. Ask Student A about what has changed at E&P.

Example: B: Have they changed their product designs?

A: Yes. They have just launched their new designs.
No, not yet. They will change them next year.

Use the information below. Make notes from Student A's answers.

E&P Future Plans
Expand office space ....
Open a new branch office in Seattle..............................
Get more sales representatives ....
Design new products ....
Do market research in Asia ....

Now change roles. You went to visit E&P. Student A will ask you what they have done. Answer Student A's questions and give details.

E&P Future plans		
Increase training programs.	✔	New training manager and more in-house courses.
Find new investment.	✘	Not yet. Still talking to banks.
Get bilingual secretaries.	✔	Six new bilingual secretaries.
Build a new factory.	✘	Waiting for investment.
Change company logo.	✘	Design company will do it next year.

4 Writing

Work in pairs. Using the notes from 3 Communication activity, write a one-paragraph report on developments at E&P Co. Ltd.
Organize your paragraph. Try to link short sentences together with *and* *but* *so* *because* to make longer sentences.

5 Exploring

Work with a partner. Talk about recent changes in your organization. Compare your ideas with another pair.

Review 3

Vocabulary 1

Match the words with a similar meaning (synonyms).

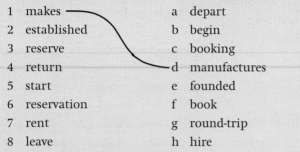

1 makes   a depart
2 established   b begin
3 reserve   c booking
4 return   d manufactures
5 start   e founded
6 reservation   f book
7 rent   g round-trip
8 leave   h hire

Language 1

Write the correct question word from the list below in each question.

| How many … | How much … | How long … | How … | When … | May I have … |

1 .... tickets do you want?
2 .... will you arrive?
3 .... nights do you want to stay?
4 .... your telephone number please?
5 .... does it take to get to your office from the airport?
6 .... your name please?
7 .... is the room per night?
8 .... would you like to pay?

Communication 1

Work in pairs. You are visiting your partner's city. Role play the situations in the boxes.
Take turns. Spin a coin to move forward. Heads = move 2 spaces. Tails = move 1 space.

| START | 1 Call the travel agent. Book a flight. | 2 Rent a car from the airport. | 3 Call your client. Confirm your appointment for 2:00 tomorrow. | 4 Ask for directions to the office. | 5 Arrive at reception. Introduce yourself. | FINISH |

Vocabulary 2

Look at the verbs in Unit 9 to find the answers to the puzzle.

Across

1 The boss is very happy because sales have .... this month.

2 The company will .... its office space.

3 The Financial Director .... the company last month.

Down

1 Sony were the first to .... the Mini disc.

2 They will .... a new store next month.

3 Next month the company will .... new staff.

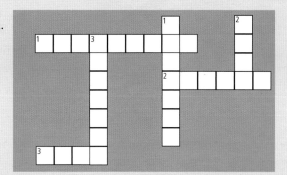

Language 2

Look at the sentences below. Which ones are correct and which ones are wrong? Explain why.

1 a The Sales Manager has left the company last month. ☐

   b The Sales Manager left the company last month. ☐

2 a The company will recruit ten new sales staff this month. ☐

   b The company has recruit ten new sales staff this month. ☐

3 a The company was established in 1978. ☐

   b The company has been established in 1978. ☐

4 a The company's sales have increased recently. ☐

   b The company's sales will increase recently. ☐

Communication 2

Work in pairs. Complete these questions to ask someone about their company.

1 .... established?

2 .... expanded recently?

3 .... 's first success?

4 .... started .... ?

Now choose one company each and ask each other the questions.

Virgin Atlantic

Virgin Atlantic Airlines was formed in 1984 by the CEO of the Virgin Group, Richard Branson. Starting with one Jumbo (Boeing 747), Virgin Atlantic flew London to New York at cut-price. It was a huge success. Virgin Atlantic now fly to many destinations around the world – from Tokyo to the Caribbean. They recently began direct flights from London to China.

Yahoo!

Yahoo! was started in 1994 by two PhD candidates at Stanford University, David Filo and Jerry Young. By 1996 Yahoo! had become so big that it was moved to Netscape's computers. Yahoo! now contains information on tens of thousands of computers linked to the web. Yahoo! has recently had new partners with interests as varied as on-line micro-surgery and multimedia cooking classes.

Routines

UNIT GOALS
- talking about what you do every day
- talking about how often you do things
- comparing your routine with others

TALKING POINT

How often do you do these things? Write every day [E], sometimes [S] or never [N] in the spaces. Ask your partner about his or her answers.

go to a restaurant for lunch ☐ bring your own lunch ☐ have a meeting ☐
talk to your boss ☐ drink coffee ☐ answer the telephone ☐

Part A   One day versus every day

1   Listening

Look at the pictures on page 49. There are two stories, but the pictures are mixed up.
Story A is what Miho Nakamura does every Monday at work.
Story B is what she did on her day off last Friday.
With a partner, separate the two stories A and B, and put the pictures in order.
The first one has been done for you.
Now listen and check your answers.

2   Vocabulary

Work with a partner. Match a word or phrase from list A with a word from list B.
Then put the phrases into the blanks under the pictures on page 49.

A		B	
had	have	my clients	the office
played	went	in front of the TV	my friend
get back	take	lunch	shopping
leave	get	breakfast	home
picked up	had	a meeting	a break
call	ate	home	tennis
take		lunch	

Now tell each other the two stories.

3 Exploring

a Make notes about something you do regularly (a routine). Now make notes about something you did on the weekend.

b Now tell each other your stories.

Routine	Last weekend
....	....
....	....
....	....
....	....

1 Brainstorming

Look at the scale below for measuring how often you do things. In groups brainstorm more adverbs to put on the scale.

0%   50%   100%

always

sometimes

never

When you can't think of any more, share your ideas with another pair.

2 Language focus

Look at the table. How often do you and your classmates do these things?
First, fill in the table yourself, then ask two classmates.

HOW OFTEN:	You	Partner 1	Partner 2
do you go home from work early?			
do you go out with your colleagues after work?			
do you entertain customers?			
do you socialize with your boss?			
do you work overtime?			
do you work through your lunch break?			
do you drive to work?			
do you take the train to work?			

3 Reporting

Tell the class about two interesting things you found out.
Example: John *always* drives to work, but I *never* do. I *usually* take the train.

4 | Culture focus

Look at the table below. Then answer the questions.

	Japan	US	UK	Germany	Canada	France
Average working hours per week ...	....	42.8	43.7	38.7*	39.2	39.6
Average years worked in one company ...	....	7.4**	8.3*	10.8++	7.9	10.4
Household savings rate ...	....	0.5	7.8	11.0	1.2	14.1

Figures for 1998 except *1997 +1995 **1996 ++1999

Source: *Japan 2000–An International Comparison* published by Keizai Koho Center, Japan Institute for Social and Economic Affairs (2000)

1   In which country do people work the longest hours? ....
2   In which country do people work the shortest hours? ....
3   In which country do people stay at one company the longest? ....
4   In which country do people save the largest percentage of their earnings? ....
5   In which country do people save the smallest percentage of their earnings? ....

5 | Listening

a   Now listen to the information about Japan. Write the answers in the table above in 4 Culture focus. Check your answers and change them if necessary.

Are you surprised by the information? Which information surprises you most? Why? Now fill in the table about yourself.

Facts	You
Average working hours per week	
Average years worked in one company	
Household savings rate (%)	

Compared to the averages on the table:
1   do you work longer hours than average?
2   have you stayed at one company longer than average?
3   do you save more or less than average?

b   Now compare your answers with your classmates.

Small talk

UNIT GOALS • informal social chat
• making conversation
• making people feel comfortable

TALKING POINT

Which topics do you find easy to talk about in English? Which are more difficult? Why do you think so? Number the topics from 1 (easiest) to 5 (most difficult).

yourself ☐   your family ☐   your interests ☐   world news ☐   politics ☐

Compare with your classmates.

Part A   Breaking the ice

1   Language focus

Look at the phrases and situations below. With a partner, decide when you would use each phrase. Check ☑ the boxes.

Meeting someone for the first time	Meeting someone you know
It's good to see you again. ☐	☑
How's business? ☐	☐
Nice to meet you. ☐	☐
I'm Dan by the way. ☐	☐
How are you? ☐	☐
Are you new here? ☐	☐
What's up? ☐	☐
How've you been? ☐	☐

2   Listening

a   Listen to two conversations. Are the people meeting for the first time in conversation 1? Are they meeting for the first time in conversation 2?

b   Listen again. Answer these questions.

1   Which of the phrases from 1 Language focus do you hear?
2   Which topics do they talk about?

food   flight   family   restaurant   sports   work   hotel

3 Reading

Small talk is informal conversation. Starting a conversation is not always easy. You should try to make the other person or people feel comfortable.

Read the two conversations below. In each conversation, when do the participants introduce themselves? Are the people comfortable? Why do you think so?

1

ANNOUNCER: There will be a short break before the next presentation. Refreshments will be served in the main hall.

AMY: Oh that was long!

JANET: Yeah. I remember him from last year. Just reads from his notes. He's always boring, don't you think?

AMY: I don't know ... this is my first annual conference.

JANET: Ah!

AMY: Do you know where I can get a drink here?

JANET: They're serving free drinks in the main hall. I'm going now. Why don't you come along?

AMY: Great. My name's Amy, by the way.

JANET: Nice to meet you. I'm Janet. This way ...

2

WOMAN: Excuse me. Sorry. Could you tell me if this is the right train for Shinjuku?

MAN: Yes it's the right train. First time in Tokyo?

WOMAN: Yeah! Are the trains always this crowded?

MAN: I'm afraid so! Actually, this isn't so bad. It's not rush hour yet.

WOMAN: I think I'll take a taxi next time. Is this Shinjuku?

MAN: Not yet. I'll let you know when to get off.

WOMAN: Thanks. ... So, how long have you been in Japan?

 Listen to the conversations. How do the people feel? Were you right?

4 Communication activity

STUDENT A: **Look at the information on page 81.**
STUDENT B: **Look at the information below.**

> Meet me at Square-Victoria station at 4:00. To get there take the subway from Mont-Royal station across from your hotel. I'll be waiting at the ticket gate.

Situation 1
You are on a train. You want to go to Square-Victoria Station. You have this note from your business associate. Ask someone if you are on the right train. Develop a conversation.

Situation 2
You are in your office where you have worked for three years in the Sales Department. You see a new face. Start a conversation, make small talk and introduce yourself.

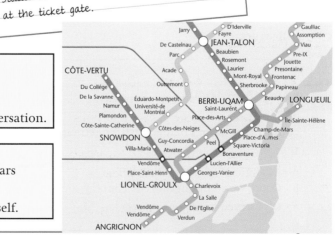

1   Listening

Yu Hon Su is in Australia on business. He is talking to Michelle Usher before they go into a business meeting. Listen to the beginning of their conversation and answer the questions below.

1 Have they met before?
2 Do they know each other?
3 How many questions does Michelle ask?
4 How many questions does Hon Su ask?
5 What topics do they talk about:

> hotels   food   television   air travel   sightseeing?

b Listen again and rearrange this part of the dialog.

YU HON SU: Uh ... I don't know ... I'll leave it up to you.

YU HON SU: At the Hotel Nikko. It's near Darling Harbour station on the metro monorail.

MICHELLE: I'd love to show you the sights of Sydney. Where are you staying?

MICHELLE: Oh yeah. I know it. How about if I meet you there tomorrow morning ... say about 11?

MICHELLE: Only your camera. We could go to the Opera House in the morning and then have lunch overlooking the harbor. Is there anything you really want to see?

YU HON SU: Sure. Do I need to bring anything?

Michelle   I'd love to show you the sights of Sydney. Where are you staying?

....

....

....

....

....

....

....

....

> In a conversation, when we are asked a question, we usually don't just answer. We also offer extra information or return a question. We call this answer + (answer plus).

In the conversation you wrote down, <u>underline</u> all the *plus* parts. Check what you chose with your colleagues.

2   Language focus

Look at the dialogs below. With a partner, write in the missing *plus* parts of the dialogs.

1
A: How was your weekend?
B: Good. We went out into the country, ate lunch by a river ... it was very relaxing. ....?
A: Oh I stayed home.

2

C: Do you still play badminton?

D: Not so often. Only about once a month these days. .... ?

C: Sure. Why not? I haven't played in ages.

3

E: How are your children? I haven't seen them in ages.

F: Fine. Owen is at university in London now. Sarah finishes high school this year. ....?

E: Donna is fine. She's working at a bank not far from home.

---

3 Communication activity

In small groups, make a list of all the words and phrases for keeping a conversation going you have found in this lesson. Now follow these instructions.

1 Write the words on the left hand side of a piece of paper.
2 On the right hand side of the paper, write a list of topics like the example below.
3 Then cut the paper into cards. You need one set of A cards for each person and one set of B cards for the group.
4 Shuffle all the cards and deal them to the members of your group.
5 Look at your cards. Start a conversation. If you use one of the A words, or talk about one of the B topics, throw down the card. Try to get rid of all your cards.

A cards	B cards
Really?	interests
Great!	family
	weekend
	home
	work

Hint: Use Answer plus (+)

---

4 Culture focus

In your country which topics are okay to talk about with business colleagues and which are not? Check the examples with a partner. If you were asked these questions, how would you feel?

Taboo questions?	comfortable	fairly comfortable	not very comfortable	uncomfortable
How old are you?	☐	☐	☐	☐
How long have you worked for this company?	☐	☐	☐	☐
Do you have children?	☐	☐	☐	☐
Why don't you have children?	☐	☐	☐	☐
How much is your salary?	☐	☐	☐	☐
Do you play any sports?	☐	☐	☐	☐
What's your religion?	☐	☐	☐	☐

Getting personal

UNIT GOALS • talking about yourself, your career and your
leisure experiences

TALKING POINT

Which of these have you done this month?

Business
given a presentation ☐
attended a meeting ☐
answered the telephone in English ☐

Leisure
played a sport ☐
eaten at a restaurant ☐
gone to a movie theater ☐

Example: I've given a presentation this month.
Compare with your classmates.

Part A   Talking about your career

1   Listening

a   Listen to Rachel Ho talking about her career. Draw lines connecting her 'stepping stones' until you reach what she is doing now.

The 'stepping stones' in Rachel Ho's business life

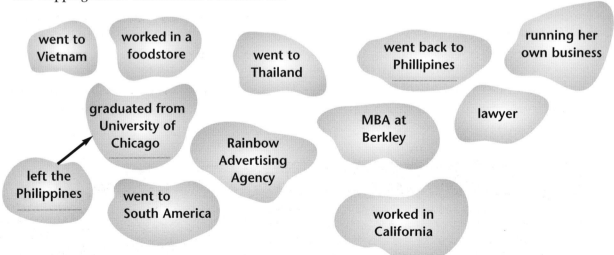

went to Vietnam

worked in a foodstore

went to Thailand

went back to Phillipines

running her own business

graduated from University of Chicago

Rainbow Advertising Agency

MBA at Berkley

lawyer

left the Philippines

went to South America

worked in California

b   Listen again. Put these dates onto the stepping stones.

   1979   1984   1995   1997

Check with a partner using the example below.

Example: In 1979 Rachel left the Philippines. In 1984 she ...

Language focus

Look at these sentences about Rachel. Write similar sentences about yourself and your partner.

1   I graduated *in* 1984.

....

2   I graduated *from* the University of Chicago.

....

3   I majored *in* Marketing.

....

4   I have been *running* my own business since 1997.
            working for myself since leaving Berkeley.

....

5   I worked *for* │ a company called Rainbow.
                  │ an advertising agency.

....

6   I worked *in* │ Chicago.
                 │ an advertising agency.

....

---

3 Exploring

Draw 'stepping stones' for yourself. Write in things which are/were important in your life.

Example: *college major, people you met, places you worked ...*

Exchange your 'stepping stones' with a partner, and tell each other about the important events in your lives. Then, in turns, stand up and tell the class.

---

4 Culture focus

Rachel went back to graduate school to study for an MBA (Master of Business Administration) after working at an advertising agency for 11 years. Do people stop their careers to study in your country/company? Look at these advertisements. With a partner, answer the questions below.

1   What kinds of course are available?
2   What kinds of people will apply?
3   How will each course benefit its participants?

4   Can you see this kind of advertising in your country?
5   Would you like to take one of these courses? Why or why not?

Heriot – Watt University MBA

The Distance-Learning MBA Program may be completed anywhere in the world. It is ideally suited to those individuals who cannot take time away from work and family to complete the degree. Study materials are fully self-sufficient and there is no requirement for tutor or student contact. Individuals may choose which and how many courses to pursue at any one time and so may pace both the workload and the costs of the program to suit their needs. A maximum of seven years is permitted to complete the degree.

University of Westminster
Certified Diploma in Accounting and Finance

▷ 1 year home study. The Distance Learning Program;
▷ An introductory weekend; Six full days of teaching throughout the year;
▷ 12 review evenings prior to the examinations; Intensive review weekend;
▷ Telephone helpline to a tutor at stated times.

1   Language focus

Talk to your classmates. Ask questions to find out the information below.
Don't forget to use *Answer +* to develop your conversations.

Who has been abroad?   Who has been on a business trip recently?
Who has lived in another town or city?   Who has changed jobs (inside or outside the company)?

Choose a new topic and ask a question. ⟶	Answer the question. Give extra information and ask a question.
Answer the question or add more information on the same topic. ⟶	Continue with an additional question on the same topic or choose a new topic …

2   Reporting

Choose one of the topics from 1 Language focus and prepare to tell the class about your experience.
Write notes below.

Example: I've been abroad three times. I went to
San Francisco in 1993 with my parents and
had a great time. The other two times were
business trips to Australia in 1998 and France
in 1999 but I still managed to do some sightseeing.

Notes

....

....

....

....

3   Listening

a   Listen to four people talking about their
personal experiences. Match the people to the topics.

scuba diving	changing jobs	living overseas	playing golf

A	B	C	D

A Tanya Martin	B Masanori Kimura	C Jason Wan	D Jenny Lin

b Listen again. Answer the questions about each dialog. Compare your answers with a partner.

Tanya Martin

1 Name two companies that Tanya has worked for.

....

....

2 Why did she change jobs?

....

Masanori Kimura

3 How often does Masanori play golf?

....

4 How long has he been playing golf?

....

Jason Wan

5 Which countries has Jason lived in?

....

....

6 How long did he spend in each country?

....

....

Jenny Lin

7 How long has Jenny been scuba diving?

....

8 Who did she meet while scuba diving?

....

---

4 Exploring

What are these activities? Have you ever done any of them? In small groups, tell each other about your experiences. Don't forget to use *Answer +*.

Now choose some topics of your own and continue telling each other about your experiences.

Review 4

Vocabulary 1

Complete the words.

1 al**ways**

2 all ___ ___ ___   ___ ___ m e

3 __ f t __ __

4 u s __ __ __ __ y

5 **a** s o m __ __ __ __ __ s   **b** f __ __ m   t __ __ __   __ o   __ __ m e

6 **a** r a r __ __ __ __   **b** n o __   o __ __ __ n

7 **a** never   **b** n __ __   a t   a __ __

Language 1

Choose a word from the list to complete each question.

> get   take   have   worked

1 What time did you .... up today?
2 You look tired! Why don't you .... a break?
3 How long have you .... for this company?
4 How long have you .... in sales?
5 Shouldn't we .... a meeting?

Communication 1

Talk to some of your classmates. Ask and answer these questions. Remember to use *Answer +* and develop a conversation (not an interview).

1 What do you usually do on weekends?
2 How long have you been living in this city/town?
3 What places have you travelled to?
4 What do you like about your job?

Vocabulary 2

There are six words or phrases to find.

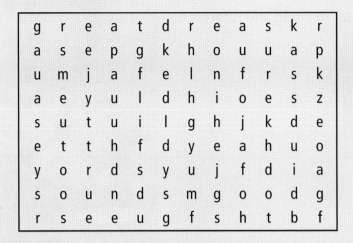

g	r	e	a	t	d	r	e	a	s	k	r
a	s	e	p	g	k	h	o	u	u	a	p
u	m	j	a	f	e	l	n	f	r	s	k
a	e	y	u	l	d	h	i	o	e	s	z
s	u	t	u	i	l	g	h	j	k	d	e
e	t	t	h	f	d	y	e	a	h	u	o
y	o	r	d	s	y	u	j	f	d	i	a
s	o	u	n	d	s	m	g	o	o	d	g
r	s	e	e	u	g	f	s	h	t	b	f

What are these words used for?

Language 2

Put the verbs in the correct tenses to complete the sentences.

1 I .... *(graduate)* in Chemistry in 1986.
2 I .... *(work)* here for 13 years.
3 I .... *(give)* this presentation in America, too!
4 I always .... *(take)* a break in the morning at 11.
5 I .... *(go)* fishing last weekend.

Communication 2

Draw 'stepping stones' for a memorable day in your life recently.

Example:

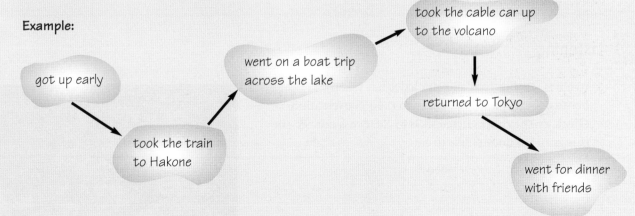

Now talk about your 'stepping stones' with a partner.

UNIT 13 Entertaining

UNIT GOALS
- recommending
- inviting and offering

TALKING POINT

What food do you like? Why? What food should visitors to your country try?

What food do you dislike? Why?

Part A   Recommending

1 Language focus

A visitor to a country is having dinner with a business associate. Check the correct ways of recommending in the box. For the items you check ☑, which response would you give?

What do you recommend?				Response
I recommend the steak.	☑	You will have the noodles.	☐	Ok, I'll have that.
The chicken is good here.	☐	I suggest the curry.	☐	Sounds delicious. I'll try it.
Eat the salad.	☐	It's up to you.	☐	I'm sorry. I don't like *(fish)* much.
How about the soup?	☐	You should try the shrimp.	☐	I'm afraid I don't eat *(red meat)*.

---

2 Listening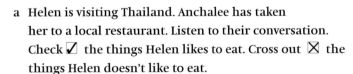

a   Helen is visiting Thailand. Anchalee has taken her to a local restaurant. Listen to their conversation. Check ☑ the things Helen likes to eat. Cross out ☒ the things Helen doesn't like to eat.

seafood	☐	salad	☐
chicken	☐	soup	☐
noodles	☐	rice	☐
spicy food	☐	sweet food	☐
red meat	☐	fried food	☐
vegetarian food	☐	raw fish	☐

b   Listen again. What three things does Anchalee recommend? Does Helen like her suggestions? Check ☑ the boxes.

1   .... ☐
2   .... ☐
3   .... ☐

3   Vocabulary

Look at the words below. Which describe how things are cooked? Which describe how something tastes? Make two lists.

sweet   spicy   boiled   sour   baked   steamed   hot   salty   broiled   charbroiled

ways of cooking something

....

....

....

....

how something tastes

....

....

....

Can you add any more?

4   Reporting

Work in pairs. Choose two dishes that visitors to your country might like to try. Write a description for each one. Use the questions below and the vocabulary in 3 Vocabulary to help you.

1   What's it called?
2   What's it made of? What's in it?
3   How's it cooked?
4   How does it taste?

1   It's called..........................
    It's made with...................
    ....
    ....

2   ....
    ....
    ....
    Report your ideas to the class.

5   Communication activity

Work in pairs. You are both in a restaurant for a business dinner.
STUDENT A: You are a visitor to Student B's country.
STUDENT B: Recommend dishes for your guest.

Student A	Student B
Say what you like or ask Student B to recommend something. Ask questions (taste? cooked? made of?).	Ask what Student A likes to eat.
Say you want it (look at 1 Language focus) or say you don't want it.	Recommend something (use your ideas from 4 Reporting if you like). Answer questions.

Now reverse roles. Student A, you are the host and, Student B, you are the visitor.

1   Brainstorming

If you visit another country, what do you like doing? Write your ideas below.

....

....

....

Compare your ideas with another student.

2   Language focus

a   Look at the invitations and offers below. Put the verbs in the correct place.

> see   go   give   show   have   take

1   Would you like to .... dinner tonight?
2   Would you like me to .... you shopping?
3   There's a baseball game tonight, would you like to .... ?
4   Would you like me to .... you a tour of our factory?
5   Would you like me to .... you around the city?
6   Would you like to .... the latest reports?

b   What questions could you ask if someone asked you the questions below?
Look at the example. Write your questions in the boxes.

Example:

A: Would you like to have dinner tonight? B: Sure. I'd love to. *Questions B could ask* What kind of restaurant ...? Where ...? What time ...?	Would you like to go to the theater tonight?	Would you like me to take you shopping?

3 Listening

a   Listen to people having the conversations in 2 Language focus. Do the speakers accept the invitations or not?

Invitation	Accept	Not accept
1		
2		
3		
4		

b   Listen again. Two of the speakers do not accept the invitation. What reasons do they give?

Reason 1: ....

Reason 2: ....

4 Communication activity

Look at your list in 1 Brainstorming. What activities can visitors to your country do? Make a list.

Example: *go to dinner, go to a museum, go shopping*

Walk around the class inviting people to do your activities.

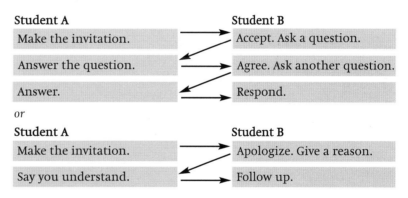

Student A	Student B
Make the invitation.	Accept. Ask a question.
Answer the question.	Agree. Ask another question.
Answer.	Respond.

or

Student A	Student B
Make the invitation.	Apologize. Give a reason.
Say you understand.	Follow up.

5 Writing

You have been sent the following two invitations from your customers. You must reply to both. Accept number 1. Do not accept number 2. Write your replies.

1

As a valued friend of Trimstein Limited we would like to invite you to our
10th anniversary party
to be held at our head office at CT Tower, Silom Road, on the 25th of November.

RSVP

2

The US Embassy

We would like to invite you to a charity dinner
and dance to be held on Saturday November 25th.

All proceeds will go to local
children's charities. Formal dress required.

$100 per person.

RSVP

Working together

UNIT GOALS
- asking people to do things
- making suggestions

TALKING POINT

What do people in your office ask you to do? What do you ask people to do?

Do you have meetings to make decisions? How often do you have meetings?

Part A   Asking people to do things

1   Culture focus

Match the situations on the left to the conversations on the right.

a Manager and clerk who know each other b Two strangers c Two friends d New manager and clerk	1 Excuse me. Could you make some copies for me please? Sure. 2 I need some copies. Ok, I'll do them. 3 Could you make some copies please? Yes, of course. 4 I need these photocopies made by three o'clock. Can you do it? Sure. I'll do them now.

In your language, is the way you talk to your boss different from the way you talk to your co-workers? How?

2   Language focus

An office manager is asking the staff to do things. Rewrite the sentences to make them more polite and less direct.

1 I want you to stay late to finish the report.
2 Call the travel agent and book a flight to Singapore.
3 Show me how to use the ATM.
4 Give me the sales figures for last month.
5 My computer has crashed. Fix it.
6 Send these letters.

Compare your answers with another pair.

Useful language

I'd like you ...
Would you mind (verb + –ing)?
Could you ...?

3 Listening

Listen to people making the same requests as in 2 Language focus. Do they say it the same way you did?

Listen again. Do the employees say 'yes' or 'no' to the requests? If they say 'no', what reasons do they give?

	Yes	No	+ reason			Yes	No	+ reason
1	☐	☐	....		4	☐	☐	....
2	☐	☐	....		5	☐	☐	....
3	☐	☐	....		6	☐	☐	....

None of the speakers actually says 'no'. What do they say instead?

4 Communication activity

STUDENT A: Look at the information on page 82.
STUDENT B: Look at the information below.

a Make these requests.
1 Ask a stranger for the time.
2 Ask an office clerk to do your filing.
3 Ask a co-worker to help you with your computer.
4 Ask your manager for a day off on Monday.

b Now respond to Student A's requests.
1 You don't have enough money.
2 Agree.
3 You have a meeting.
4 Agree.

5 Writing

Work with a partner. Write an email to MBMG and request a company brochure and information on health insurance for your international staff.

MBMG INTERNATIONAL

Financial Services

We offer the best in:
→ Financial planning
→ Tax advice
→ Health insurance

Contact Phil Taylor: **387-9999**
ptaylor@mbmg21.com

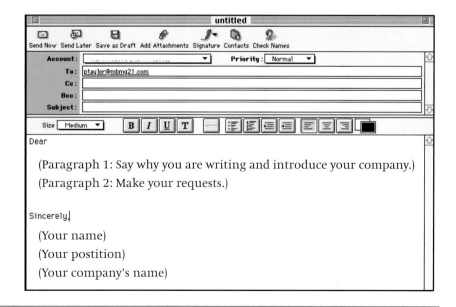

Dear

(Paragraph 1: Say why you are writing and introduce your company.)
(Paragraph 2: Make your requests.)

Sincerely,

(Your name)
(Your postition)
(Your company's name)

Part B   Making suggestions

1   Culture focus

How often do you have meetings? Does everyone talk in the meeting?
Do you have an agenda? Do you make decisions in the meeting?

Read these quotes. One is from an Asian working in an American office.
The second is from an American working in an Asian office. Are your
meetings like either of these?

Meetings are very difficult
for me here in the US. We are expected
to discuss issues and make decisions right there and
then. I prefer to go away and think about the issues,
and then talk to my co-workers and my boss
about them. I don't like to argue
with my co-workers.

Meetings are very
boring here. My boss just
talks everyone and tells us
what he wants us to do. I
never get to speak and give
my opinion. I have ideas but
no one wants to discuss
them in the meeting.

Useful language

Polite suggestions
We could ...
Why don't we ...?
Let's ...
How about + *–ing* ...?

2   Language focus

You are having a meeting to discuss new ways to market
your company's products. Use the ideas to make suggestions.

Ideas

1   Advertise on TV ....

2   Visit stores and ask them to have a special display ....

3   Have a contest to win prizes ....

4   Make a new website ....

 Now listen to the meeting and compare it to what you wrote.

3   Listening

Listen to the meeting in 2 Language focus again. Number the responses 1 to 4 as you hear them.

Yes, but ...   ☐   I agree, but ...   ☐

That's a good idea.   ☐   Yes, I think I will.   ☐

I agree.   ☐   That's a good idea, but ... ☐

Check your answers with another student.

4   Communication activity

Work with a partner to make these short conversations.
Your company's sales are falling and the company is in trouble.

1 Student A Make suggestions   **Student B** Respond

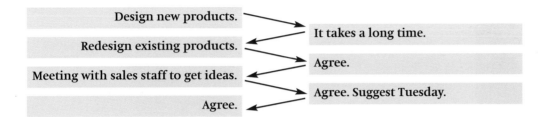

Design new products.

Redesign existing products.

Meeting with sales staff to get ideas.

Agree.

It takes a long time.

Agree.

Agree. Suggest Tuesday.

Now reverse roles.

2 Student B Make suggestions   **Student A** Respond

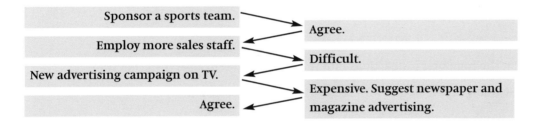

Sponsor a sports team.

Employ more sales staff.

New advertising campaign on TV.

Agree.

Agree.

Difficult.

Expensive. Suggest newspaper and magazine advertising.

5   Exploring

Work in small groups. Your boss has decided that all the staff will go on a trip together for one day.
You have the responsibility for planning the trip. Have a meeting to decide the following things.

                                    Notes

1   Where will you go? Why?   ....

2   How will you get there?   ....

3   What activities will you do?   ....

4   What / Where are you going to eat?   ....

Make suggestions and try to reach an agreement. Make notes about your decisions.
Report your decisions to the rest of the class.

UNIT 15

Getting help

UNIT GOALS
- showing people how to do things
- talking about problems

TALKING POINT

What did people show you to do when you joined your company? What was new to you?

When you have a problem at work, who do you talk to? Do people ask you for help?

Part A	Showing how to do things

1 Listening

Work in pairs. Put the computer instructions into the correct order to answer the question.

How do I perform a simple calculation with the calculator on my computer?

a   enter the first number   ☐

b   click on Calculator   ☐

c   click =   ☐

d   select Programs and point to Accessories   ☐

e   click + to add, − to subtract, * to multiply, or / to divide   ☐

f   enter the second number   ☐

g   click on the Start button   ☐

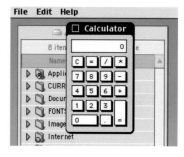

Listen to someone give the instructions. Check your answers.

2 Language focus

Complete the instructions for using a photocopier. Choose one adverb and one verb from the lists to complete the sentences.

Adverbs	Verbs
Next	lift
Then	close
First	enter
Finally	put
After that	press
Next	take
Then	put

1 .... , ... the lid.

2 .... , ... the paper face down on the glass.

3 .... , ... the paper in line with the marks.

4 .... , ... the lid.

5 .... , ... the number of copies you want.

6 .... , ... the green button to start.

7 .... , ... your copy and the original.

3 Communication activity

STUDENT A: Look at the information on page 82.
STUDENT B: Look at the information below.

a   Write instructions on how to use an ATM.
    Then tell Student A how to use an ATM.

Automated Teller Machine.

b   Listen to Student A tell you how to send a fax. Make notes as you listen.

 Now listen to someone explain how to use an ATM and how to send a fax. Check your answers.

4 Exploring

Work in pairs. Can you explain to each other how to do the things below?

Excuse me. How do I ...
get an outside telephone line?
transfer a call to another extension?
put paper in the photocopier?
print out an email message?
work the coffee machine?
call a cell phone from my desk?

Now walk around the class asking people how to do these things. Ask a different person each time.
Explain to any student who asks you. Make notes.
Compare your answers with a partner.

1   Reading

Read about four of the employees at Aikon Ltd.

Sarah Wurz is the Office Manager. She's in charge of all the clerical staff. She is also responsible for organizing office maintenance and ordering office supplies and furniture. She is very friendly and easy to talk to.

Jane Lee is the Marketing Manager. She is in charge of the sales representatives and the publicity department. She is always busy and she is difficult to get hold of. She has a lot of meetings and she is often out of the office with clients.

James Grant is the computer technician. He looks after all the office P.Cs and maintains the network. Most of his time is spent looking after the warehouse stock computers. He's young and very popular with all the employees.

George Walker is the Warehouse Manager. He supervises the stock levels in the warehouse. He also arranges all the orders to be sent to the customers. It is always busy in the warehouse and George has many employees working for him.

Look at the statements below. Which employee at Aikon Ltd. should each person talk to? Use the verbs below to help you.

ask	tell	go and see	talk to

Who should I talk to?

I need to know last month's sales figures. **Example:** *You should ask Jane Lee.*
I can't finish my sales report by Friday.
I want a new chair in my office.
A customer told me his orders are always delivered late.
My email doesn't work.
I need some samples to show to customers.
I need to know how much we can spend on advertising.

2   Brainstorming

Work in pairs.
If someone had the same problems in 1 Reading in your company, who should they talk to?
Compare your answers with another pair.

Useful language

If you don't know the person's name, use *someone* or *somebody*.
Example: Tell someone in the Sales Department.
Ask somebody in Administration.

3 Listening

Read the responses below then listen to the tape. What are the problems? Make notes.

Problem	Response
1	You should ask your manager.
2	You should go and see the Marketing Director. He'll tell you.
3	You should tell your secretary.
4	You should talk to all the staff.

Compare your answers with a partner.

4 Communication activity

Work in pairs. A new employee has just arrived in your office. Think of five problems he/she might have on the first day. Write your ideas below.

1 ....

2 ....

3 ....

4 ....

5 ....

Walk around the class and tell your problems to other students.

Listen to other students' problems and offer help.

5 Culture focus

Read these complaints from managers from around the world in inter-cultural situations. Answer the questions below.

1 Have you experienced similar complaints?

2 What do you think the problem is in each case?

3 Can you make suggestions to the managers below?

a
The staff don't talk to me until it's too late. For example, I give them a job to do and they wait until the deadline to tell me they can't finish it.

c
The staff are always arguing with me when I ask them to do something. Why don't they just do what I ask them to do?

d
The staff always ask me to make quick decisions, if they want a day off work, for example. Why don't they give me time to think about it? Why do they always have to push me?

b
The staff always say 'yes' when I ask them to so something, even if they can't do it.

Review 5

Vocabulary 1

Match the verbs on the left with the nouns on the right.

1	go	a	a fax
2	send	b	dinner
3	take	c	the theater
4	have	d	shopping
5	send	e	an email
6	type	f	a message
7	go to	g	a letter

Language 1

Decide if these are offers (O) or requests (R).

1 Could you go to the post office please? ☐
2 I'd like you to type this letter for me. ☐
3 How about going to dinner tonight? ☐
4 Would you like me to take you shopping? ☐
5 Would you mind sending this fax please? ☐
6 Would you like to go to the theater? ☐
7 I'd like to take you to the National Museum. ☐

Communication 1

Write down things you would like to do this week.
Walk around the class inviting your classmates to do things with you.
Listen to their invitations. Accept or decline. Write in the schedule if you accept.

Monday	Friday
Tuesday	Saturday
Wednesday	Sunday
Thursday	

Vocabulary 2

Make a list of the things you do at work.

Example: write reports, answer the telephone, …

With a partner, tell each other what you wrote.

Listen to your partner's list. Write down what you hear.

Your list   **Your partner's list**

....

....

....

Language 2

Change the following to questions.

Example: I can't find any paper. Where is it?

1   I need to speak to Mr. Chou. Do you know .... ?
2   I'm hungry. .... go to lunch?
3   I need to send an urgent letter. .... type it for me?
4   I don't know how to use this machine. .... showing me?
5   I want to find out about the new design. .... should I talk to?

Communication 2

STUDENT A: **Look at the information on page 82.**
STUDENT B: **Look at the information below.**

Tell Student A how to shut down your computer. Use the notes to help you.

Close
Start button
Shut down
Wait
Turn off

Student A Communication activities

Unit 2　Part A 4 Communication activity page 11

You have a picture of the same office as Student B, but there are ten small differences. Can you find them? Tell Student B about your picture and listen to Student B talk about his/hers. Use the language in 3 Language focus to help you.

1　...
2　...
3　...
4　...
5　...
6　...
7　...
8　...
9　...
10　...

Unit 2　Part B 4 Communication activity page 13

Listen to Student B explain the locations of Fizco in China. Mark the locations on the maps below.

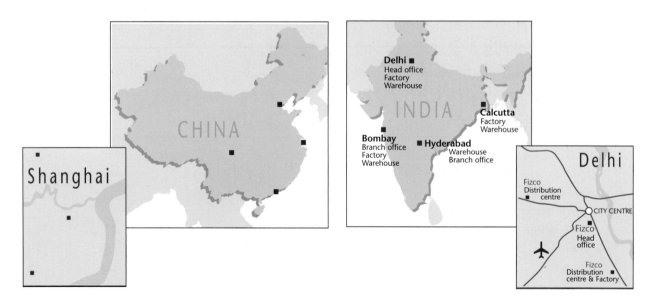

Now look at the maps of Shanghai and China above. The maps show the location of Fizco work places in China. Explain the locations to Student B.

Unit 3 Part A 3 Communication activity page 15

a Listen to Student B describe the Sharp AR 200
photocopier. Fill in the missing information.

  type: Digital .... copies
  speed: .... copies per minute
  capacity: .... sheet paper tray
  price: $ ....

b Describe the Hewlett Packard Office Jet Pro 1170Cxi Multifunction to
Student B. Use the phrases below to help you.

It is ...
It has ...
It can ...
You can ...
It costs ...

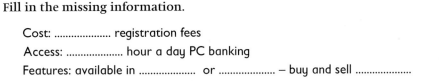

- copier, printer, scanner and fax
- digital color copies
- black and white – 9 pages per minute, color – 3 pages per min
- 150 sheet paper cassette
- $ 499

c Listen to Student B describe Citibank's CitiDirect Internet Banking Service.
Fill in the missing information.

  Cost: .... registration fees
  Access: .... hour a day PC banking
  Features: available in .... or .... – buy and sell ....
  foreign currencies on-line

d Describe the Bank of Scotland's Offshore Account to Student B.

- The Offshore Service is for expatriates and international investors only.
- 24 hours a day telephone banking
- no tax on interest

Unit 4 Part A 5 Communication activity page 21

STUDENT A: **In your local time, when is the best time to call:**
a Michael Devas
b Marcel Marquez?

Now ask Student B when the best time is to call:
a Julie Edwards
b Sharon Davies.

Example: A: When's the best time to call Julie Edwards?
  B: Well, you can call her between (time) and (time) but don't call her (say when).

Unit 5   Part A 2 Communication activity page 25

Situation 1
You are Professor Harold Buchowski of the University of Michigan. Take a call.
Make a note of who called you.

Situation 2
You are Ms. Rena Burling of Yamanaka Industries, Singapore Sales Office. Call Yamanaka
Industries Head Office in Japan and ask to speak to Mr. Hideo Takanashi.

Situation 3
You are Ms. Yuko Ueno of Chock-a-Block Toys Ltd. You are in the office with two other people,
Mr. Eric Lum and Ms. Eriko Sato. Take a call. Answer in your own language at first.
Make a note of who called you.

Situation 4
You are Mr. Ravi Singh of Singh and Son Ltd. Call the International Bank of Shanghai,
and ask to speak to Ms. An-Li Wang.

Unit 5   Part B 2 Communication activity page 26

Situation 1
You are John Rees of Heiwa Life Insurance.
Call Industrial Air Conditioning Limited.
Ask them to send you a brochure
for office air conditioners.

Situation 2
You are Wasan Sukucharoen of Jupiter
Printing Company. A customer calls.
Fill in the form.

HEIWA LIFE INSURANCE

JOHN REES
MAINTENANCE MANAGER

2-5-15 Ogikubo, Suginami-ku, Tokyo

Customer request form

print brochure ☐   list ☐   visit ☐
quotation ☐   other ( ) ☐

Name: ....

Address: ....

Tel: ....

Fax: ....

Email: ....

Request: ....

Notes: ....
....

Unit 6   Part B 3 Language focus page 31

Choose a complaint from the list below. Student B should choose an apology and action from his/her list. You should then choose a follow-up.
Now change roles.

Example: **Complaint** *I was promised a 10% discount but I only got 5.*
Apology *I'm sorry about that.* **Action** *I'll check with the salesperson and get back to you.*
Follow up *Thanks.*

A

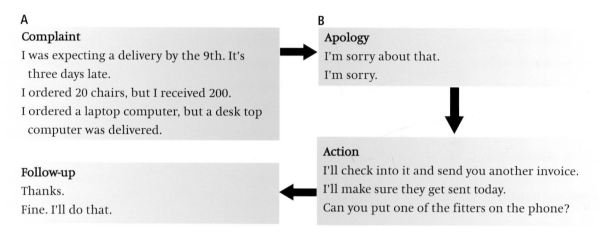

Complaint
I was expecting a delivery by the 9th. It's three days late.
I ordered 20 chairs, but I received 200.
I ordered a laptop computer, but a desk top computer was delivered.

Follow-up
Thanks.
Fine. I'll do that.

B

Apology
I'm sorry about that.
I'm sorry.

Action
I'll check into it and send you another invoice.
I'll make sure they get sent today.
Can you put one of the fitters on the phone?

Unit 6   Part B 4 Communication activity page 31

Situation 1
Look at the computer catalog and the invoice you sent to Student B. Student B will call to complain about a mistake on your invoice. Apologize and offer to take some action.

COMPUTER WORLD
INCREASE YOUR MEMORY

Rewritable CD Drive	$450.00
Superdisk Drive	$280.00
MO Drive (230MB)	$210.00
Zip Drive	$199.00
Rewritable 600MB CDs (5 pack)	$55.00
Superdisk (3 Pack)	$28.95
MO Disk (230MB)each	$ 7.55
Zip Disk (10 Pack)	$95.95

Invoice	
1 X Zip Drive XC250AM	$280.00
Zip disk (10 pack) R2200X	$ 95.95
	$375.95

Situation 2
Look at the order you sent and the invoice you received from Student B. Find the mistake, then call Student B and complain.

ORDER	
	12 x desk AM25P
	1 x executive desk AM40E
	12 x swivel chairs PJ25P
	1 x executive chair Pz90E

INVOICE		
12 x desk AM25P	$292.00ea	$3504.00
1 x executive desk AM40E	$628.00ea	$ 628.00
20 x swivel chairs PJ25P	$ 62.90ea	$1258.00
1 x executive chair Pz90E	$252.80ea	$ 252.80
		$5642.80

Unit 7   Part A 4 Communication activity page 35

Situation 1

You want to stay in the Park Hotel next week for three nights with your husband/wife/partner. Call Student B at the Park Hotel and make a reservation for a double room.

Situation 2

You work for 'First Travel' travel agency in New York. Student B will call you to book a flight. Take his or her reservation. Ask questions and fill in the form. (Only China Airlines is available at these times at $679 one way or $989 round trip.)

China Airlines		
Name :		
Date ....March	**time**	16.30
from New York	**to**	....
Flight # CHA01		

Unit 8   Part A 4 Communication activity page 39

You are a visitor to Fukuoka. Student B is a clerk at Akasaka station. Ask Student B how to get to these places.

Fukuoka Airport   **Meinohama**   **Kaizuka**

Make notes.

Now you are a clerk at Qianmen station in Beijing. Student B is a visitor to Beijing. Answer his or her questions.

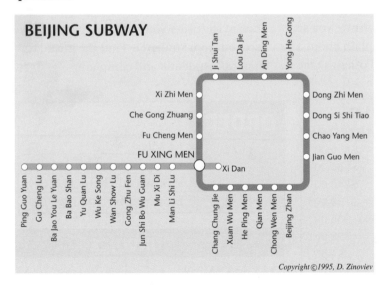

BEIJING SUBWAY

Copyright ©1995, D. Zinoviev

Qianmen Station
Platform 1 – to Donsishitiao
Platform 2 – to Fuxingmen

You have just returned from a visit to E&P Co. Ltd.. Student B will ask you what has changed at E&P.

Example
B: Have they changed their product design?
A: Yes. They have just launched their new designs.
No, not yet. They will change them next year.

Use the information below. Answer Student B's questions and give details.

E&P Future Plans

Expand office space	✓	An extra floor in the office building.
Open a new branch office in Seattle	✗	Not yet. Will open next month
Get more sales representatives	✓	Two new representatives in each branch.
Design new products	✗	Not yet. Will go into production next year.
Do market research in Asia	✓	Completed on time. Results are interesting.

Now change roles. You went to visit E&P. Ask Student B what they have done. Make notes about Student B's answers.

E&P Future Plans

Increase training programs	Get bilingual secretaries ....
Find new investment	Build a new factory ....
	Change company logo ....

Unit 11 Part A 4 Communication activity page 53

Situation 1
You are on a subway train (the red line), currently at Mont-Royal heading for Lionel-Groulx. Someone will ask for help. Develop a conversation.

Situation 2
You have just joined a new company. You will be working in the Personnel Department. Start a conversation, make some small talk and then introduce yourself.

Unit 14　Part A 4 Communication activity page 67

a　Respond to Student B's requests.

1　You don't have a watch.

2　Agree.

3　You don't know about computers.

4　Agree.

b　Now make some requests. Student B will respond.

1　Ask a co-worker to lend you $10.

2　Ask your manager to check a letter you wrote.

3　Ask your assistant to go to the Post Office.

4　Ask your co-worker to show you how to use the photocopier.

Unit 15　Part A 3 Communication activity page 71

a　Listen to Student B tell you how to use an ATM.
Make notes as you listen.

b　Write instructions below on how to send a fax.
Then tell Student B how to send a fax.

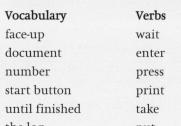

cashpoint

Automated Teller Machine.

Useful language

Vocabulary	Verbs
face-up	wait
document	enter
number	press
start button	print
until finished	take
the log	put

　Now listen to someone explain how to use an ATM and how to send a fax. Check your answers.

Review 5　Communication 2 page 75

Tell Student B how to search for Cambridge University Press on the internet. Use the notes to help you

> www browser
> search engine (e.g. Yahoo!)
> type Cambridge University Press
> click
> click on link

Language file

Introducing yourself

Written English	*Spoken English*
My name is ...	My name's ...
I am ...	I'm ...
I am from ...	I'm from ...

Introducing other people

This is ...   He is ...   She is ...

These are ...   They are ...

Talking about yourself

I'm from ...

I live in ...

I studied/I am studying at college

I majored in ...

Match the parts to make six sentences.

My name's	Seattle in the U.S.
I'm from	the Human Resources Department
I'm working in	Rick Howe
I'm	
I'm in	
I come from	

Language file

Prepositions of location

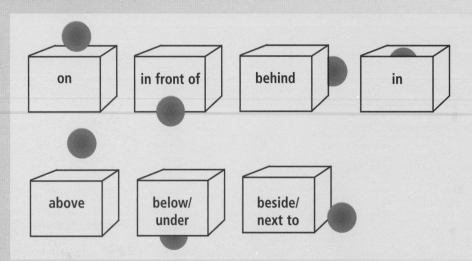

Where's the clock?

Do you have an eraser?

Where's Mr. Jones' desk?

Can I have some letter size paper?

Where are the reports?

Do you have some scissors?

It's above the filing cabinet.

Yes. It's on my desk.

It's next to the window.

Yes. It's under the printer.

They are on the desk in front of you.

Yes. They are on the table you.

Vocabulary file

Office equipment

Which of these things do you have on or in your desk? Which do you have in your office? Write *office* or *desk* next to the things you have.

whiteout ....

eraser ....

computer ....

fax machine ....

coffee maker ....

stapler ....

ruler ....

filing cabinet ....

telephone ....

printer ....

lamp ....

electric socket ....

clock ....

scissors ....

paper ....

monitor ....

book shelf ....

calculator ....

telephone directory ....

drawers ....

glue ....

paper clips ....

files ....

pictures ....

plants ....

whiteboard ....

Work places

Match the picture to the type of work place.

> plant   office   factory   laboratory   warehouse

Which does your company have?

Unit 3 Help folder

Language file

Describing a product or service

It is ...   It has ...   It can ...
You can ...
(company name) makes ...
We make ...
(company name) provides ...
We provide ...
(company name) produces ...
We produce ...

Make sentences using *provide* or *make* for the following companies:

1 Pepsi ....
2 Citibank ....
3 Toyota ....
4 Amari Hotels ....
5 (your company) ....

Comparing things

... is bigger than ...

... is more expensive than ...

big	bigger
cheap	cheaper
quiet	quieter

expensive	more expensive
economical	more economical

Vocabulary file

Adjectives

big small cheap expensive economical exciting boring practical slow fast
attractive comfortable near to far from close

Using 3 different words from the Vocabulary file, make three sentences about things you own.

For example: My car is slower than a Toyota Celica

- ....
- ....
- ....

Unit 4 Help folder

Language file

Telling the time around the world

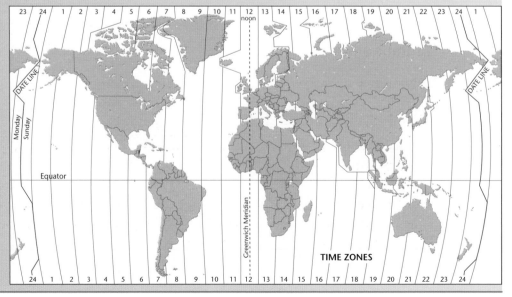

Internet domain names often include a two-letter country code at the end. The US does not have a code. Match the codes below to the countries. What is the time difference between these countries and yours?

Domain	Country	Time difference
1 th	a South Africa	....
2 fr	b Japan	....
3 za	c Israel	....
4 de	d Malaysia	....
5 au	e Thailand	....
6 my	f Germany	....
7 ru	g Russia (Moscow)	....
8 sg	h Australia (Sydney)	....
9 jp	i France	....
10 il	j Singapore	....

Telling the time

18:45 — eighteen forty-five or
six forty-five or
quarter to seven

12:10 — Twelve ten or
ten past twelve or
ten after twelve

14:00 — fourteen hundred (hours) or
two o'clock or
two p.m. or two

20:30 — Eight thirty or
half past eight or
half eight or
thirty after eight

07:00 — oh seven hundred (hours) or
seven o'clock or
seven a.m. or seven

How many ways can you say these times?

| 10:15 | 17:35 | 02:07 | 11:50 | 16:30 | 06:00 |

Language file

Prepositions

Look at the example text below.

> The meeting is *at* eleven thirty. The presentation is *for* two hours. The tour is *from* four o'clock *until* / *to* five thirty.

Now fill in the blanks with the correct preposition.

The presentation starts [1] .... one o'clock and lasts [2] .... two hours. There will be a coffee break [3] .... three o'clock [4] .... three thirty.

Language file

Asking for details

Can I Could I May I	have your	name? fax number? telephone number? address?

Checking

Can I Could I May I	read that back to you? just check that please?

Could you Can you	spell that please? spell that for me please? repeat that please?

Offering help

How can I help you?
What can I do for you?

Stating reasons for calling

I'm calling to I'd like to	request a brochure. arrange a meeting.

Complete the dialog. Write in the missing parts for person A.

A: KBK, ... help .... ?
B: Hello. Can I speak to John Dwyer please?
A: Who ....?
B: Madeline Xiang
A: ....spell ....?
B: X-I-A-N-G
A: Just .... through.
B: Thank you

Language file

Countable nouns

a lot of	
many	chairs
three	telephones
a few	drinks
not many	disks
not a lot of	
some	

Uncountable nouns

	tape
a lot of	information
some	trouble
not much	glue
not a lot of	news
	money

Are these words countable or uncountable?

paper   newspapers   desks   staff

When do you use *How much ... ?* and
when do you use *How many ... ?*

Language file

Ordering

I want to place an order for ...
I'd like to order ...

Dealing with problems

There | are two problems with the invoice.
      | is a mistake on ...

I ordered ... | but I got ...
I was promised ... |

Apologizing for problems

I'm sorry about that.

What seems to be | wrong?
                 | the problem?

Put this dialog in order.

A: Not at all.

A: I'm sorry about that. I'll check it for you. May I have your account number please?

B: Yes. My name's Kay Johnson of MicroX. I placed an order last week and it hasn't arrived yet.

B: MX343467

A: Hello, Unifit. Can I help you?

A: Just a moment please ... Ms Johnson. Your order went out yesterday. You should receive it later today.

B: Goodbye

B: Oh. Thank you.

A: Bye.

Language file

Asking for something

		book a room.
I want	to	make a reservation.
I'd like		rent a car.
		order a taxi.

Vocabulary file

Booking a service

Hotel

What kind of room would you like?
single / double / twin room

How many nights do you want to stay?
Five nights.

When do you want to stay?
From 5th March until 9th March.

What time can I *check in*?
When do I need to *check out*?

Car rental

small car / family car   one day   12 hours

Flight

leaving   check-in counter   flight number

Hotel	Car Rental	Flight	Restaurant
single room	small car	leaving	table for two
double room	family car	check-in counter	
five nights	one day		
check-out	12 hours		

Add these words to the lists above. You can add some words to more than one list.

breakfast included   twin room   check-in   flight number   fully booked   business class   sedan   4-door

Language file

The Imperative

When giving instructions (e.g. directions) it is not necessary to use a subject in the sentence.
Follow the example to change the directions below. Try to link the sentences together like this.

.... and .... or .... , ... and ....

Example: First you go straight. Then you should turn left at the bank.
→First go straight and then turn left at the bank.

1   You take the train to Ginza. Then you change to the Marunouchi line. ...

....

2   You take the street across from the station. You walk straight up the street until you see the bank.

....

3   You turn left. You walk 100 meters. Our office is on the right. ...

....

Vocabulary file

Department names
Check the departments in your company. Write the name of the department in your own language.

Accounts		
Research and Development (R&D)		
Human Resounrces (HR) or Personnel		
Sales		
Marketing		
Administration (Admin)		
Technical		
Engineering		
Advertising		
Design		
Distribution		
Production		
Customer services		

Can you add any more to the list?

Language file

Conjunctions

Look at the sentences below. Decide which conjunction to use.

and	but	so	because

1   Sales grew 20% last year .... the company has recruited two extra sales staff.
2   The sales figures have increased .... everyone worked hard.
3   The Customer Services department has recruited more staff .... moved to a bigger office.
4   The accounts have been finished .... the President hasn't seen the report yet.

and (+)
The company has recruited two designers. A new Personnel Manager has joined the company.
The company has recruited two designers *and* a new Personnel Manager.

The company has built a new factory. The company has opened a new showroom.
The company has built a new factory *and* opened a new showroom.

but (-)
The company has opened a new branch *but* sales have not increased.
The company has launched new products *but* they don't have new catalog yet.

so (=)
The company has expanded the office *so* they can recruit more staff.
The company has recruited new sales representatives *so* they can increase sales.

because (=)
The company has built a new factory *because* the old one was too small.
or
Because the old factory was too small, the company has built a new one.

Vocabulary file

Complete the table. Check you know the verb endings.

	Past tense (for past tense)	Past participle (for present perfect)
make	made	made
begin	began	begun
found		
start		
hire		
leave		
join		
sell		
manufacture		
develop		
expand		
recruit		
establish		
increase		

Language file

Talking about routines

Something happens regularly. For example, every day.

Simple present tense

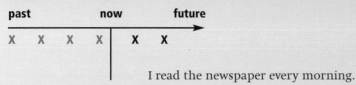

I read the newspaper every morning.

Talking about past events

Something that happened once. For example, last week.

Simple past tense

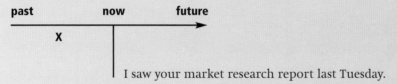

I saw your market research report last Tuesday.

Choose the correct tense for the verbs in the sentences below.

1 I .... *(give)* a presentation last Thursday.
2 She usually .... *(watch)* the news in the evening.
3 I sometimes .... *(talk)* to foreign clients in English.
4 I don't usually bring lunch to work, but yesterday I .... *(do)*.

Vocabulary file

Adverbs of frequency

always / all the time   often / usually   sometimes / from time to time   rarely / not often   never / not at all

Common verb partnerships

| go | out
home | | get | up
home
back | | take | the train
a break | | have | a meeting
a meal
a drink
coffee
lunch | | make | plans
an
appointment |

Can you think of any more 'partners' for these verbs?

Unit 11 Help folder

Language file

Keeping a conversation going

Answer plus (+)

When someone asks you a question, makes a request or offers an invitation, a simple answer is fine. But if you want to develop a conversation, add something extra after your answer.

Examples

(Question) How long have you been working here?
(Answer) Five years. (plus) How about you?

(Question) What do you think of the sales forecast?
(Answer) It's good. (plus) The computer graphics are excellent, don't you think?

Write (*Answer*) and (*plus*) for each of the following questions:

1 Where are you staying?
(Answer) .... (plus) ....
2 What do you do at weekends?
(Answer) .... (plus) ....
3 What did you think of the presentation?
(Answer) .... (plus) ....

Vocabulary file

Keeping a conversation going

Really! Me too! Yeah. Sounds good. Great. I'd love to!

Unit 12 Help folder

Language file

Talking about continuing circumstances

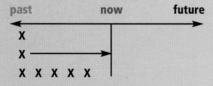

past   now   future

I went to the Philippines five years ago.
I have been living in the Philippines for five years.
I have been playing golf every weekend for five years.

Vocabulary file

Talking about your career

to graduate	in English from University
a graduate	of Harvard University

	company	time period
worked for	IBM Walmart	five years 2 months

	Place
worked in	San Francisco
worked at	a garage a superstore

Complete these sentences with the appropriate tense of the verb

1 I .... (*graduate*) in law 12 years ago.

2 I .... (*work*) here since 1993.

3 I .... (*go*) to the UK to attend graduate school in 1996.

4 I .... (*live*) in Seoul now for 6 months.

5 I .... (*train*) as an engineer in California until 1998.

6 I .... (*work*) in advertising since I graduated

Unit 13 Help folder

Language file

The Passive voice

Often the subject is unknown or unimportant. In this case the Passive voice *is* often *used* in English.

Be + verb + past participle

Examples:

Subject | Object
|
The chef makes *the soup* from coconut milk and chilli powder.
The soup is *made* from coconut milk and chilli powder.
|
Object | be verb+pp

The cook fries the chicken with ginger.
The chicken is fried with ginger.

Try these

1 Thai people use shrimp and lemon grass for this soup.

....

2 Everybody must cook these dishes slowly.

....

3 These dishes must be cooked slowly.

....

Vocabulary file

Make a list of ten things you like to eat. Draw a line to the way they are cooked.
Draw another line to the way they taste.

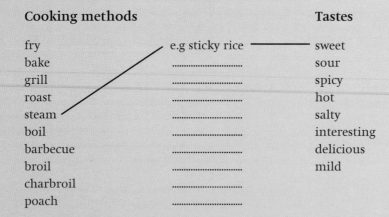

Cooking methods		Tastes
fry	e.g sticky rice	sweet
bake	....	sour
grill	....	spicy
roast	....	hot
steam	....	salty
boil	....	interesting
barbecue	....	delicious
broil	....	mild
charbroil	....	
poach	....	

Language file

Accepting an invitation

Would you like to go to dinner?	Sure. I'd love to.
	Yes. That sounds great.

Declining an invitation

	pause	apology	reason
Would you like to go to dinner?	... Oh.	I'm sorry.	I have another appointment this evening.

Unit 14 Help folder

Language file

Asking people to do things

A: I'd like you to *type* this letter for me please.
A: Could you *type* this letter for me please?
A: Can you *type* this letter for me please?
A: Would you mind *typing* this letter for me please?

B: Sure.
B: Yes, of course.
B: Yes, I'll do it now.
B: No. I'll do it right away.

A: Could you *type* this letter for me please?

B: Yes, but I have to finish this report. I can type your letter after that.

A: Would you mind *typing* this letter for me please?

B: I'm sorry, but I have to go to a meeting now. I'll type it as soon as I come back.

Note: 'Would you mind...?' questions are answered 'No' if you can do the request.

Make a list of everyday requests people ask you or you ask them.

....

....

....

....

....

Making suggestions

We could recruit more sales staff to visit clients.
Why don't we recruit more sales staff to visit clients?
Let's recruit more sales staff to visit clients.
How about recruiting more sales staff to visit clients?

Vocabulary file

Match each of the verbs with one of the nouns.

type	the email
make	a letter
send	the filing
prepare	a telephone number
write	the database
get	a report
check	the computer
do	an email
update	copies
back-up	an invoice

Language file

The Imperative

The imperative was first looked at in Unit 8 to give directions. The imperative is also used in this unit to explain how to do things. Don't forget, it's okay to leave out the subject when giving instructions.

Example:

~~You~~ enter your PIN* number.

~~You~~ put the document face down.

* PIN Personal Identification Number

Vocabulary file

Fill in the missing verb. Choose from the list below.

> Go and see / talk to / tell / ask

1 a) I just received a complaint from our biggest customer.

   b) You should............................... them. Meeting them will make them feel better.

2 a) How do I find out if an order has been sent?

   b) I'm not sure. Why don't you .... Arnold? He might know.

3 a) Excuse me. Could I .... you for a few minutes? I need to ask you something.

   b) Sure. Have a seat.

4 a) Our supplies are coming late every week. Do you think I should .... the manager?

   b) Sure. She needs to know.

Transcripts

Unit 1 New faces

Part A   **1 Listening**

LUCY:	Hello ... is this your first day?
ANDREW:	Yes. Uh ... my name's Andrew Walsh. I'm joining the Sales Department.
LUCY:	I'm Lucy Chang. Call me Lucy.
ANDREW:	Nice to meet you Lucy.
LUCY:	Good to meet you too. Where are you from, Andrew?
ANDREW:	I'm from Phoenix, Arizona, but I've been living in California since I was in college.
LUCY:	Oh ... what did you study?
ANDREW:	I majored in Economics. How long have you been here, Lucy?
LUCY:	Seven years. I was in the Sales Department for six years ... now I'm in the Human Resources Department.
ANDREW:	Oh ...
LUCY:	Anyway. Nice to meet you. If you need anything, let me know.
ANDREW:	Sure. I'm looking forward to working here.
LUCY:	Bye.
ANDREW:	Bye.

4 Culture focus

PERSON A:	My name is Koji Hirano. All of my colleagues call me by my last name, Hirano. Usually we add 'san' to names in Japan. For example, my boss, Toru Nakamura, is always Nakamura-san and he calls me Hirano-San ... unless he's angry with me and then it's just 'Hirano'.
PERSON B:	Everyone at the office calls me Pamela. My boss, new employees, everyone. My last name is Bryson, but usually only visiting sales people call me Ms. Bryson.
PERSON C:	My name is Elisabeth Reiser. My friends and colleagues call me Eli but I really prefer my whole first name, Elisabeth.

Part B   **1 Listening**

A:	Mr. Haneda, I'd like to introduce you to Joshua Travis. Joshua works in the Marketing Division of our company. Mr. Haneda is a Director of Yonegawa Industries.
B:	It's nice to meet you, Mr. Haneda.
C:	Nice to meet you too. How long have you been at International Foods, Mr. Travis?

Unit 2 Around the office

Part A 2 Listening

1 A: Excuse me?

B: Sure.

A: I need something but I don't know what it's called in English.

B: Umm.

A: It's for drawing a straight line.

B: Oh, you want a ruler. There's one on my desk. I'll get it for you.

A: Thank you.

2 A: Oh no! I've made a mistake on my report. Do you have ... er ... some white stuff ... to fix my mistake.

B: You mean whiteout. Sure. We keep it in the cupboard. I'll get you some.

A: Thanks.

3 A: Can you help me?

B: Sure.

A: I'm doing my expense report and I need ... er ... you know, it's a thing for adding numbers ... with buttons and a screen.

B: Oh yes, a calculator. Sure. There's one over there next to the fax machine.

Part B 3 Listening

Kanda Motors Thailand now has a new factory producing cars for export to Australia and New Zealand. The factory is located on the outskirts of Ayuttaya City, which is about 100 km north of Bangkok. They also have a factory producing cars in the south of Thailand near Hat Yai. Motorcycle production is at the Khon Kaen factory in the northeast in the region known as Esarn. The company's Head Office is in the suburbs of Bangkok in the east of the city. They also have a branch office in Chiang Mai in the north. They have showrooms in the centers of most Thai cities.

Unit 3 Products and services

Part A 2 Listening

MEE SUN YANG The Xerox XC-1875 is a black and white photocopier. It can make 18 copies per minute and has a 700 sheet paper capacity. It can reduce copy size down to 64% or can enlarge up to 156%. The basic model costs $2799.

HARVEY GIL mbanx Direct is Canada's first direct bank. You can do your everyday banking transactions 24 hours a day, 365 days a year through your personal computer, telephone and ATM. With mbanx, you can speak to someone, no matter what time it is. mbanx on-line has account information, money transfer and other services available to account holders. Please call 800 555 1111.

Asian Airways flies direct to more cities than any other airline. On Asian Airways, seats in economy class have more space so you can relax while you fly. Asian Airways offers a better choice of meals and drinks. So ... does all this mean we're more expensive than other airlines? No. It doesn't.

Asian Airways. Better service. Better value.

Unit 4 Time zones

Part A   4 Listening

SPEAKER 1: Hi! My name's Michael Devas, and I'm from New York City. The trains here are always crowded in the morning, so I go to work late and leave late. I leave home at 8:30, when the trains are OK, and I start work around 9:30. I usually have lunch at one o'clock, which means I have a long afternoon. I leave my office at about 7:30. I sometimes work on Saturdays when we are busy.

SPEAKER 2: I'm Marcel Marquez. I live in Madrid, Spain. I'm the sales manager for a carpet-making company. I start work at 9:00 am. My company is very traditional, so we all have lunch at 2:00 pm. The factory and offices close for siesta time. Because we have a long break, we don't finish until 8:00 pm. I sometimes go to my office on Sunday afternoons because it is so quiet that I can get a lot of work done.

SPEAKER 3: Hi my name's Sharon Davies and I'm a graphic artist from L.A. I love my job because it's very flexible. I try to start work at 09:00, but I usually get there at 10:00. I always go to lunch at 1:00 because my friends' schedules are not flexible. I guess I leave work at about 6:00, but sometimes later. I don't go to the office on weekends because I can take my work home, if I need to.

SPEAKER 4: I'm Julie Edwards from Florida. I work for a company which builds small boats. I'm the Personal Assistant to the Managing Director. She likes to come in early to work, so I have to start at 8.00. I like to eat a sandwich for lunch at my desk, usually at 12.00, but sometimes I have to go to a resturant with the boss. I leave work at 5.30 everyday and I never work on weekends because my company doesn't want to pay overtime.

Unit 5 On the phone

Part A   1 Language focus

1

(ring)

A: Hello, Mitchell Designs.

B: Can I speak to Ms. Sampson please?

A: Speaking.

B: Ah. Hello. My name is Peter Rogers of ....

2

(ring)

A: East Asia Credit Bank. Can I help you?

B: Hello. Ms. Pitsamai Keree's office please.

A: Who should I say is calling?

B: Julianne Hunter.

A: Just a moment. I'll put you through.

3

(ring)

A: Kansai Rayon de gozaimasu.

B: Uh .... hello .... do you speak English?

A: Yes, a little.

B: My name is Mel Douglas of Trenchard Carpets. Can I speak with Mr. Jyoji Matsuo please?

A: Just a moment please.

Part B 3 Listening

1

A: Hello. Jupiter Printing Company. Can I help you?

B: Hello. My name is Mai Kurihara. I'm calling from Marketing Services in Japan. I have your new print brochure, but it doesn't have prices in it. Could you send me this year's price list by fax please?

A: Sure. Could I have your name and fax number please?

B: Yes. My name is Mai Kurihara ...

A: ... Uh ... Could you spell that please?

B: Yes. Mai, M–A–I. Kurihara, K–U–R–I–H–A–R–A

A: Thanks. And the fax number?

B: Yes. The code for Japan is 81 and the number is 6 ... 8644 ... 3900.

A: 6 ... 8644 ... 3900.

B: Uh ... can you fax it to me today please?

A: Certainly. I'll do it immediately.

B: Thank you.

A: Bye.

B: Bye.

2

A: *(in Japanese)* IAC de gozaimasu.

B: Uh ... do you speak English?

A: Yes. This is Industrial Air Conditioning. Junko Takahashi speaking. How can I help you?

B: Uh ... could you send me this year's brochure for air conditioners please?

A: Certainly. Are you interested in office or factory air conditioners?

B: Office.

A: OK. Can I have your name and address please?

B: Yes. It's John Rees of Heiwa Life Insurance. The address is 2-5-15 Ogikubo, Suginami-ku, Tokyo.

A: Ok. Let me just check. John Rees of Heiwa Life Insurance. The address is 2–5–15 Ogikubo, Suginami-ku, Tokyo.

B: That's right.

A: I'll get the brochure in the mail to you.

B: Thank you.

A: Bye.

B: Bye.

Unit 6 **Placing an order**

Part A   **1 Listening**

a

KAY:	Do you have a minute?
SUNG-HO:	Sure. What's up?
KAY:	I'm ordering clothing from Unifit. Is there anything you need?
SUNG-HO:	Uh, yeah. We need a few labcoats.
KAY:	How many?
SUNG-HO:	Er, three ... four ... six ... should do it.
KAY::	Anything else?
SUNG-HO:	Goggles. We need lots of goggles, like 20 pairs.
KAY:	OK, six lab coats and 20 pairs of goggles.
SUNG-HO:	Thanks Kay.
KAY:	No problem.
KAY:	Ron. I'm putting together an order of clothing. Need anything?
RON:	Yeah. We have a new employee so he needs three sets of overalls...
KAY:	... OK
RON:	...and gloves ... about 30 pairs please.
KAY:	What kind of gloves?
RON:	Like these.
KAY:	Oh. OK.
RON:	Uh ... that's it, I guess.
KAY:	Thanks Ron.
RON:	See you.

b

A:	Unifit. Can I help you?
B:	I'd like to place an order please.
A:	Do you have an account with us ma'am?
B:	Yes. The account number is MX 343467.
A:	MicroX Corporation. Ms. Johnson. Is that correct?
B:	Eh ... yes.
A:	How can we help you Ms. Johnson?
B:	Uh ... I'd like to order 30 lab coats – item number P21G5.
A:	30 lab coats.
B:	Uh huh ... how much are they?
A:	$25 each.
B:	OK. And overalls. Item number P2251. How much are they?
A:	$43 each. How many do you need?
B:	25.
A:	25 pairs of overalls. OK.
B:	And goggles. 50 pairs of item number WB91.
A:	50 pairs at $2 a pair. Anything else?
B:	Er ... 50 pairs of S32 gloves ... uh, that's it.
A:	The gloves are $1.50 a pair. Is that okay?
B:	Yes, that's fine.

A: OK. Can I just check your order Ms. Johnson?

B: Sure.

A: That's 30 lab coats – item number P21G5, 25 pairs of overalls – item number P2251, 50 pairs of goggles – item number WB91 and 50 pairs of gloves – item number S32.

B: Yes.

A: Will that be all Ms. Johnson?

B: Yes. Thank you, that's fine.

A: OK. We'll send the goods immediately and invoice you as usual. Is that OK?

B: Yes, that will be fine.

Part B   **2 Listening**

A: Electric Supplies. Customer Service Division. Emily speaking. How can I help you?

B: Uh … My name's Paula Xiang. I'm calling from Supersaver Supermarkets. I've just received delivery of the goods I ordered. There are two problems with your invoice.

A: Oh … what seems to be wrong Ms. Xiang?

B: Well the first problem is that I was promised a 10% discount, not 5.

A: Oh, I'm sorry about that. I'll confirm that with the sales person and send you a new invoice.

B: Thank you.

A: Was there another problem?

B: Yes. I ordered 10 fluorescent light strips but I've got 20 here. The delivery truck is still here …

A: OK. Put 10 back on the truck. I'll make the changes to the invoice and send it to you immediately.

B: Thank you. You've been very helpful.

A: Not at all.

B: Bye.

A: Bye.

Unit 7 Making a reservation

Part A   **2 Language focus**

RECEPTIONIST: Park Hotel. Can I help you?

ALEX: I'd like to make a reservation please.

RECEPTIONIST: Certainly. When will you be staying?

ALEX: From Thursday June 20th until the 22nd.

RECEPTIONIST: OK so two nights.

ALEX: Yes.

RECEPTIONIST: Would you like a single room or a double?

ALEX: A single room is fine.

RECEPTIONIST: A single is $140 a night.

ALEX: OK.

RECEPTIONIST: And may I have your name please?

ALEX: It's Alex Meyer

RECEPTIONIST: Could you spell that please?

ALEX: Alex. A L E X. Meyer is M E Y E R.

RECEPTIONIST: Thank you. And can I have your telephone number?

ALEX: Sure. It's London 020 9696 514.

RECEPTIONIST: Thank you very much Mr. Meyer. Your reservation has been made for a single room for June 20th for two nights. My name is Julie.

ALEX: Thank you very much.

RECEPTIONIST: Bye.

ALEX: Bye.

3 Listening

AGENT: STA. James speaking. Can I help you?

LUCY: Uh ... I'd like to reserve a flight one-way to Tokyo please.

AGENT: When will you be flying, ma'am?

LUCY: Tomorrow. March 4th.

AGENT: There is a flight with North East Airways on the 4th leaving Los Angeles at 11:05 a.m.

LUCY: Mmm ... That's fine.

AGENT: Can I have your name please?

LUCY: Lucy Zhang.

AGENT: Could you spell your last please?

LUCY: Sure. It's Z H A N G.

AGENT: How will you be paying, Ms. Zhang?

LUCY: By Credit card. The number is 4535 1567 3765 4354.

AGENT: Ok, Ms. Zhang. Can I confirm your booking? You will be flying with North East Airways to Tokyo leaving Los Angeles tomorrow at 11.05. Please pick up your ticket from the check-in counter. Please remember to check in two hours before the flight time.

LUCY: Thank you very much.

Part B 2 Listening

AGENT: JFK Airport Car Rental Service. How can I help you?

ANGEL: My name is Angel Tan. I'm arriving at JFK on the 22nd of April. I'd like to rent a car.

AGENT: Sure. How many days do you want the car, Ms. Tan?

ANGEL: Let me see. I'm flying back on the 25th ... so three days.

AGENT: OK. And what kind of car would you like?

ANGEL: Well, I don't really know American cars .... I'll be in the States on business. I need a car that I can take customers in.

AGENT: Well, we have a mini-van available with a driver if you need ...

ANGEL: Oh no. I don't need anything that big. Just a four door sedan is fine.

AGENT: How about a Nissan Maxima?

ANGEL: That's fine. How much is it?

AGENT: $95 per day, plus gasoline. Do you want me to reserve it for you?

ANGEL: Yes please.

AGENT: OK. And can I have your fax number? I'll fax you a form to fill in and the details of the rental agreement.

ANGEL: Sure. My fax number in Singapore is 2563 298.

AGENT: That's 2563 298. (Uh huh) Thank you Ms. Tan. Bye.

ANGEL: Thank you. Goodbye.

Unit 8 Getting around

Part A 3 Listening

1

Walk to the end of the street and turn left. Go straight until you reach the station. Take a train from platform 1 and change at Tokyo station. Take the Marunouchi line one stop to Ginza. Ask someone for the building when you get there.

2

Take a taxi from outside and tell the driver to take you to the Landmark Hotel. Go out of the hotel and turn left. Walk along the street and the office you want is in the second building on the right.

3

Walk across the street to the station. Take a train to Shibuya and get off there. Go outside the station and take a bus to the office. The driver can take you right to the door.

Part B 2 Listening

1

A: Good morning can I help you?

B: Good morning. My name's Lu-Ann Chan from Active Industry. I'm here to see Yoko Yoneyama.

A: Do you have an appointment?

B: Yes at 10 o'clock.

A: One moment please. I'll call Ms. Yoneyama. Please take a seat.

B: Thank you.

2

A: Hi. Can I help you?

B: Hello. I'd like to see Mr. Smith please.

A: What department is that?

B: Sales department. I have an appointment at 2 o'clock.

A: Can I have your name please?

B: Denise Chapman from AsiaPac Limited.

A: Thank you. Please wait while I tell Mr. Smith you're here.

B: Thank you.

Unit 9 About the company

Part A 1 Listening

Steve Wozniak and Steve Jobs met in high school. After working in Silicon Valley for a few years, Wozniak made a computer which later became the Apple 1. Steve Jobs decided they could sell it. On April 1st, 1976 they launched the Apple Computer, and by 1980 they had several thousand employees. In 1984, Apple developed the first Macintosh computer.

Apple Computer had mixed fortunes in the 1980s and early 90s, but things picked up with the arrival of the iMac. This low-end computer sold more than any other in late 1998. Apple continue to lead the way with innovative design.

Unit 10 Routines

Part A **1 Listening**

MIHO: I'm a sales manager for Seido cosmetics. Mondays in the sales office are always the same. I leave home at seven because I start work early, usually at eight. We always have a sales meeting on Monday morning. For the rest of the morning I call my clients to make appointments. I always take a break around eleven and usually have coffee. My boss and I take a late lunch and make plans for the week. In the afternoon I go out and start making sales calls. I usually don't get back to the office until after six, so I often don't get home until after seven. Mondays are long days.

MIHO: I had a great day last Friday. I slept in until after ten. I had coffee and fresh French bread for breakfast on the balcony outside because it was a beautiful sunny day. I drove to town and picked up my friend Sachiko. We had lunch at a pizza place and then went to our tennis club. I played tennis with Sachiko and two friends for about two hours. On the way home, I went shopping. I bought food for dinner. At home, I cooked 'yakisoba' a Japanese fried noodle dish, and ate in front of the TV while I watched my favorite TV show. I had a very relaxing day.

Part B **5 Listening**

In Japan, the average work week has fallen from 43 hours per week in 1988 to 38.8 hours in 1998. The average length of time worked in one company is 11.3 years. The average Japanese household saves 13.6 percent of its income.

Unit 11 Small talk

Part A **2 Listening**

1

SARAYA: Hi. Are you new here?
JAYAN: Yeah. How did you know?
SARAYA: Uh, you look nervous. I'm new too. First day?
JAYAN: Mmm. How about you?
SARAYA: Last week. I'm Saraya by the way.
JAYAN: I'm Jayan. Nice to meet you Saraya.

2

RUTH: Hi Marika. It's good to see you again.
MARIKA: Ruth! How've you been?
RUTH: Fine. Where are you staying? At the Hilton?
MARIKA: No. I'm at the Holiday Inn. The Hilton's full.
RUTH: Hey, that's great! The Holiday Inn is right near my house. Come over for dinner one evening while you're here, OK?
MARIKA: I'd love to! I get so tired of hotel food. How is your family? I bet the kids have grown. ...

MICHELLE:	Hello. Mr. Yu?
YU HON SU:	Yes?
MICHELLE:	Michelle Usher. We've talked on the phone ...
YU HON SU:	Ah. Ms. Usher. Nice to meet you in person.
MICHELLE:	Thank you for coming. Did you have a good flight?
YU HON SU:	Pretty good. This is a very impressive building.
MICHELLE:	Mmm. Is this your first time at the head office?
YU HON SU:	Yes. It's my first time in Australia actually.
MICHELLE:	Really! Well, if you have any free time while you're here, I'd be happy to show you around.
YU HON SU:	Oh, I don't want to bother you.
MICHELLE:	Not at all. I'd love to show you the sights of Sydney. Where are you staying?
YU HON SU:	At the Hotel Nikko. It's near Darling Harbour station on the Metro Monorail.
MICHELLE:	Oh yeah. I know it. How about if I meet you there tomorrow morning ... say about 11?
YU HON SU:	Sure. Do I need to bring anything?
MICHELLE:	Only your camera. We could go to the Opera House in the morning and then have lunch overlooking the harbor. Is there anything you really want to see?
YU HON SU:	Uh ... I don't know ... I'll leave it up to you.
MICHELLE:	Great ... OK. We're here.

Unit 12 Getting personal

Part A   **1 Listening**

Rachel Ho

Hi, I'm Rachel Ho. I left the Philippines in 1979 to go to the United States of America to study. I studied Marketing at the University of Chicago and graduated in 1984. After graduating, I worked for an advertising agency called Rainbow. After 11 years I left Rainbow to go back to school. I studied business and got my MBA from the University of California at Berkeley. I graduated in 1997 and came back to the Philippines to start my own advertising company. I've been running my own business since then.

Part B   **3 Listening**

Hi. I'm Tanya. I'm from Detroit. I've been living and working in LA for five years now. I work for AT&T. When I lived in Detroit, I worked for a small company called Genius Software. I left that company to join AT&T in Seattle because the salary was much better. I asked to transfer to LA five years ago.

I'm Masanori Kimura – or Masa for short. I love playing golf. I've been playing for 19 years, but I'm not getting any better. I only play once a month because I'm so busy at work.

My name's Jason. Jason Wan. I'm from Taiwan originally, but I've been living in Saipan for two years. I work here as a chef. I'm lucky because I trained in Paris for three years. French chefs can always get jobs easily in hotels in Asia – even if they're not French!

Hi. I'm Jenny. I'm from Hawaii. I've been scuba diving all my life. I go diving every chance I get – on weekends, vacations, even at night! These days, I usually go with my husband. I met him while scuba diving in Australia!

Unit 13 Entertaining

Part A   **2 Listening**

ANCHALEE: What would you like, Helen?

HELEN: I'd really like to try some real Thai food.

ANCHALEE: Is there anything you don't like?

HELEN: Well, I don't eat much red meat, but chicken is OK. I love seafood.

ANCHALEE: How about spicy? Can you eat spicy food?

HELEN: Sure. But not too spicy please.

ANCHALEE: OK. How about starting with some Tom Yam Goong.

HELEN: What's that?

ANCHALEE: It's a spicy soup made with lemon grass and chilli. You can have it with chicken or shrimp.

HELEN: Yes I think I've heard of that. I'll have the shrimp.

ANCHALEE: OK. And what about some chicken fried with cashew nuts? It's eaten with plain rice.

HELEN: Sounds great.

ANCHALEE: And beef with oyster sauce?

HELEN: Sorry. I don't eat red meat I'm afraid.

ANCHALEE: I'm sorry. I forgot. How about a nice red snapper?

HELEN: A whole fish?

ANCHALEE: Yes. They grill it with pepper and garlic.

HELEN: That would be great.

ANCHALEE: Good. We can finish off with some fresh fruit.

Part B   **3 Listening**

1

A: Would you like to have dinner with us tonight?

B: Sure. I'd love to. What time?

A: 6.30. We can pick you up at your hotel.

B: Great. What kind of restaurant are you thinking of?

A: How about a very nice Chinese restaurant near here?

B: Sounds good.

2

A: Would you like to go to the theater tonight? I've got some tickets.

B: ... Oh, I'm sorry. I've arranged to meet some old friends tonight.

A: No problem. Maybe next time you come.

B: Yes. That would be nice.

3

A: Are you busy tonight?

B: No. I don't have anything planned.

A: Would you like me to take you shopping?

B: Oh, no, thank you. I'm very tired. I'd like to stay in my room tonight.

A: Of course. Let me know if you want to go somewhere.

B: I will. Thank you.

4

A: There's a big soccer game tonight. Would you like to go?

B: Yes. I'd love to. Who's playing?

A: It's a match between Arsenal and the Thai national team.

B: Great. Sounds good.

A: We'll need to leave here about 5:30.

B: Fine, I'll be ready.

Unit 14 Working together

Part A   3 Listening

1

A: Would you mind staying late to finish the report?

B: I'm sorry, but I have plans tonight. I'll come in early tomorrow to finish it.

A: That's fine.

2

A: I'd like you to call the travel agent and book a flight to Singapore for me please.

B: Sure. What are the details?

3

A: Could you show me how to use the ATM please? I can't figure it out.

B: Of course. Would you like to go now?

A: Yes please.

4

A: Could you give me the sales figures for last month please?

B: Yes. I'll get them now.

A: Thank you.

5

A: My computer has crashed. Could you fix it please?

B: I'm sorry, I'm not very good with computers. I'll call a technician for you.

A: Thank you.

6

A: Would you mind sending these letters please?

B: I'm sorry, I have meeting now. Can I send them at lunchtime?

A: Yes, that's fine.

Part B   2 Listening

A: Does anyone have any new ideas for marketing the new products?

B: Well ... how about advertising on TV? It's the most effective way.

C: Yes, but we don't have the budget for it. TV is far too expensive.
    I was thinking we could visit stores and ask them to have a special display of our new products.

A:	That's a good idea. I like that. Any more suggestions?
C:	Why don't we have a contest to win prizes?
B:	I agree, but the prizes would need to be special, and that's expensive too.
A:	Yes we need to do some research on that. Any more?
C:	Let's build a new website to launch the new products. We could find ways of attracting people to the site.
B:	I agree. I think it's important to have a separate website for these products.
A:	Fine.

Unit 15 Getting help

Part A   1 Listening

To perform a simple calculation first, click on the Start button. Then select *Programs* and point to *Accessories*. Next click on *Calculator*. Enter the first number and then click *plus* (+) to add, *minus* (−) to subtract, *star* (*) to multiply or *slash* (/) to divide. Next enter the second number. Finally click *equals* (=).

3 Communication activity

1

A:	Excuse me, but could you show me how to use an ATM please?
B:	Of course. First insert your card in the slot. Then enter your PIN number. Next select 'Withdrawal' and enter the amount. Wait. Take your money. Finally take your card and receipt.
A:	Thank you.
B:	You're welcome.

2

A:	Could you show me how to use the fax machine please?
B:	Sure. First put the document in the machine face down. Then enter the fax number you want. Next, press the start button. The machine will dial automatically. Wait until the document is finished going through the machine. Finally you can print out a report.
A:	Easy. Thank you.
B:	Sure.

Part B   3 Listening

Problem 1
My friends are going on vacation next month and I want to go with them.
Problem 2
I need to know how much we can spend on advertising.
Problem 3
My email doesn't work.
Problem 4
My department's telephone bill is very high.

Acknowledgements

We are grateful to our readers, whose detailed and constructive comments were extremely valuable to us. We would especially like to thank James Hunter, Hyogo, Japan; James Boyd ECC, Japan; Todd Odgers TCLC, Japan; Nien-Hung Lu, Ging Chung Business College, Taiwan; Laurence Earnshaw, Ramkamheng University, Thailand; Jeffrey Paschner, AUA Language Centre, Thailand; Gordon Robinson, Nanyang Technological University, Singapore; Matt Budd, Nihon Schering K.K., Japan; Lori Solbakken, Lado Management Consultants Ltd, Taiwan.

At Cambridge University Press, we would like to extend our warm thanks to our Commissioning editor, Will Capel, and our Editor, Sally Searby, whose expertise and guidance helped us overcome any difficulties. Our thanks also go to Janaka Williams and Debbie Goldblatt for their expert suggestions.

Gareth Knight is grateful to his colleagues at the Department of Linguistics, Srinakharinwirot University and ThaiTESOL for their support and understanding, and to his wife, Sasithorn, for her patience.

Mark O'Neil would like to thank the long-suffering members of his family in Japan who gave up their time to enable him to work on this project – his children, Talia, Clare, Kieran and Morris and his wife, Soko.